PRAISE FOR
The Point Is in the Purpose

"In *The Point Is in the Purpose*, readers are invited to move beyond the chaos of busy schedules and surface-level success to discover what truly drives fulfillment. With clarity, wisdom, and practical insight, this book challenges you to realign your daily actions with 10 tools to find your greater purpose. Whether you're leading a real estate team, building a business, or simply seeking more meaning in your day-to-day life, this book offers a refreshing roadmap to doing work that matters—and living a life that resonates. **A must-read for anyone ready to trade the grind for grounded, purpose-driven impact.**"

— JIM BEACH,
speaker, radio host, and bestselling author of School for Startups

"**This isn't just another take on purpose. Brent brings humility, real-life experience, and a practical framework that truly hits home.** His 10 for 10 story is more than a great moment, it's a model for consistency, focus, and living with intention. This book delivers what most leadership reads miss: no corporate jargon, no surface-level advice - just honest reflection, actionable insight, and a clear reminder of what really matters."

— MEGAN AMODIO,
Senior Director of Training & Operations Services, Huddle House

"I have heard Brent Rittersdorf give his 10 for 10 presentations at several local business luncheons and am always impressed by the attentiveness and the engagement of the crowd. Brent is a people person and the greatest networker I have ever known. **I have seen the ripple effects these steps have had on the lives of people in our community. I highly recommend this book. Brent Rittersdorf is a flat-out winner.**"

— MARLON LONGACRE,
Community Pastor of Piedmont Church

"In high school, Brent was not the most skilled player on the team but he was disciplined and coachable, which is why he had to play. He was always in the right place at the right time, and every team needs players who are willing to do the little things the right way over and over again. **Those are the values he teaches in this book.**"

— DAVE COOK,
former Basketball Coach at Rockland District High School

By weaving his personal stories and challenges into every one of the shots, Brent's insights are real and authentic. He gives readers a true understanding of where commitment comes from."

— FARRELL MIDDLETON,
owner and President of The Bell Curve of Life and author of A Performer/A Environment

"**This book encapsulates Brent and his deep understanding of helping others live more thoughtfully and intentionally.** Any reader will understand what he is 'pouring' out and be able to relate it to their own lives. I'm very honored to have met Brent and heard about Bronson, as well as how he helped Brent discover his purpose. It's rewarding to watch Brent take his 10 shots on this journey."

— JOHN SILVEY,
Director of Operations for Southeastern Fastpitch and former Member of the Year for the Marietta Business Association

"What's your purpose? It seems like an easy thing to answer, but it's really not for most people. The first time Brent asked me, I was caught off-guard and didn't really know how to answer. Brent's 10 for 10 does a phenomenal job outlining not only why finding your purpose is important, but also provides guidelines and examples of how to handle everything that life throws at you. *The Point Is in the Purpose* is humble yet inspiring, and funny yet motivational. **It speaks to the many challenges we all go through in adult life while trying to make a living and make something of our lives.**"

— GREG FULLER,
former General Manager of Six Flags Atlanta Properties

"For so many people, the search for purpose in our lives is a never-ending journey. Sometimes it is crystal clear, but in other moments our passions and pursuits become a bit more hazy, clouded by the circumstances of life. Brent takes readers from a single identifiable moment in his life, in this case, a high school basketball game, to show how you can define your purpose, identify it, and take steps to actually achieve it."

— CHRIS CARPENTER,
Managing Editor, Crossmap.com

"Brent has poured his heart and soul into exploring what it really means to live with purpose. **Every page feels like a conversation with a trusted friend who's not afraid to challenge you, inspire you, and walk alongside you as you seek your own path.** This isn't just a book about finding purpose – it's a book written by someone who lives it."

— BILL GOWLANOCH,
Director of Operations for IHOP

THE *point* IS IN THE PURPOSE.

THE *point* IS IN THE PURPOSE.

How Going **10 for 10** Can Change Your Life

BRENT RITTERSDORF

Published by Ripples Media
www.ripples.media
Atlanta, GA

First printing 2025

Cover design by Lyn Asman
Book interior by Najdan Mancic

ISBN 979-8-9931418-0-0 Paperback
ISBN 979-8-9931418-1-7 Hardback
ISBN 979-8-9931418-2-4 eBook

Library of Congress Control Number: 2025920709

TABLE OF CONTENTS

FOREWORD

reat, another book about finding your Purpose. In a seemingly endless world of self-help books and feel-good themes, why read another book about Purpose? Because this one is different, this one connects us—it is written with, well ...*Purpose*.

The Point is in the Purpose is the adventure we have all been on. The highs and lows, the struggles, the big wins, the good times and the bad. Brent gives the reader a guidebook on how to define and identify Purpose and not lose sight of where they are in the process of going 10 for 10. The practical application of each shot in the 10 for 10 framework keeps the reader not only engaged, but helps them understand where they are in the process of their own story—or if they have *even taken* the first shot.

Brent takes you on a journey through his experiences, his successes, and his failures and he does it from a viewpoint from which we can all relate. His *real world* stories paint a picture of how to realize your Purpose without having to have some major life event or achievement that's destined to be picked up by Hollywood, like finishing a grueling endurance race or selling a startup for millions of dollars. By his own admission, Brent is an otherwise ordinary guy, with a framework to help readers make small changes that will have an extraordinary impact on their lives. He does not introduce a high-minded boardroom concept, and then sends you out to figure it out on your own. Rather, as you read through this book and start reflecting on the Purpose in your life, he follows it up with a step-by-step guide on what to expect next. This book provides a practical application of fulfilling Purpose in your daily life. A refreshing, as well as convincing aspect of this book, is ownership. Brent paints a great picture of how the influence of others can impact many areas of your life, but ultimately you are the one responsible. *No one else can take the shot for you.* In a world filled with the influence of others, positive or negative, this book brings you back to the foundation of self-discipline. You are responsible for the shots you take—no one else. You then surround yourself with people who will support you on the journey. It offers great insight and I wish more books would say it this plainly.

Brent's story of how he first discovered his Purpose with his beloved dog Bronson relates to the reader so easily as we all have similar moments in life or relationships that shape us more than we realize. So many of the examples in this book could be snapshots taken out of anyone's life, Brent was just courageous enough to write it down in hopes it might help someone else along the way.

Promise, Practice, and Accomplishment. Three pillars that define so many areas in our lives, and Brent relays that to the reader in a way that is free from pretense and corporate *guidance* of what others say you should feel. We should all lean more into these three pillars on a daily basis and I am sure these messages will resonate with many of you reading this book. Understanding something is only part of the battle. Actually doing something about it is what gives it meaning.

I started my entrepreneurial journey around the same time Brent started his real estate business. We were two people new to the game, trying to define what Purpose and process really means. I have had the pleasure of calling him a friend all this time and have enjoyed a front-row seat watching him develop the 10 for 10 model over the past years. His journey in writing this book is just as exciting as the message within. Having retired from the military, I like processes. They are definable, testable, communicable, and repeatable. I like the way Brent laid this out in his book so well that I had him speak to a group of future military leaders as they were preparing to earn their commissions and become officers in the National Guard. His message of finding your Purpose and going 10 for 10 adapts regardless of industry or job title, making it simple to apply these lessons learned to your own life.

In my own business journey, Brent has been a great sounding board for my crazy ideas. His passion for this book has certainly helped shape my business over the years.

To everyone reading this book, go in with a ready mindset as you may find yourself on a different trajectory than you were expecting. If you follow his 10 for 10 process, though, you have an excellent shot at ending up where you ultimately need to go.

Dave Young,

Maj, USA (Ret.)

INTRODUCTION

Solving the Purpose Problem

The buzzer went off for the final time in the fourth quarter of the high school basketball game, and a new buzz began. The Bangor Auditorium was filled with craziness on that cold February day in Maine. We had won the basketball game, but I had won something so much more. I had no idea it would change my life, other than the coach coming up to me and screaming, "Brent! You went 10 for 10!"

Everyone I know has a favorite number. Mine is 12. It was always my favorite number growing up, even before a certain NFL quarterback wore it and won a lot of Super Bowls, and became an icon, especially for those of us who grew up in New England.

Most people I know have a favorite word as well. I have one too, but it's more like a curse at times because it's all-consuming. The word is *PURPOSE*. I self-proclaim to own the word. I have thought and studied its principles and power my whole life, from the days in high school, to my career in Corporate America, to my second career in sales, and the development of this book. Many people have favorite words they like to use in casual conversation, but I breathe it, explore it, taste it, and reflect on it. In fact, I *never* stop thinking about it.

Why do people love talking about Purpose? Pay attention to the next PowerPoint presentation you experience, and chances are you will see the word *Purpose* in that presentation somewhere. I look for that word and when I see it, I perk up to see what they will say about the word and how it affects them, only to be left disappointed because they just glance over the word, thinking it speaks for itself.

It left me wondering why the word that is so powerful and used so often is left open-ended. I concluded that perhaps the reason why is that while you want to have Purpose, find Purpose, and live Purpose, *most people don't truly know what their Purpose is*. It's nice that all those PowerPoint presentations have the word *Purpose* inserted next to a cute graph or picture, but it stops there. The presentation may leave the audience with a nice message, but it falls well short of helping people actually identify and internalize their *Purpose*. They continue their search, hoping that the next time they see the *SMART* goals sheet, or some other graph, it will help them find their Purpose.

I tested my conclusion further by simply asking people: "What is your Purpose?" The awkward looks and responses of deflecting the question only fueled my conclusion above. If you like, try asking someone the question and you will see the same awkward looks. Maybe even look at the person in the mirror and see what looks back at you.

We have a Purpose problem.

On some level, aren't we *all* striving to find our Purpose? Or at least, improve on it? Certainly, we all know someone who is trying to identify theirs. Think of all the people post-pandemic who participated in the Great Resignation. Or all the people today who are Silent Quitters in the workplace. Or all the people who left their jobs to start their own gig. Or all of the people surfing the internet *right now* searching for the next thing.

We have a Purpose problem, and the solution doesn't exist by glancing at the word in a PowerPoint.

This book isn't just about finding *Purpose*, but identifying a practical framework to actualize it and live it out. My goal with this book is to take this term that everybody talks about at a level of 30,000 feet and make it relevant. We're constantly told to look at things, especially in business, from a birdseye view. However, in this case I want you to be "all in" at the ground level so that this high level buzzword becomes a daily companion.

At its core, you really have to ask the question: What is *your* Purpose, and how do you balance all of the events that include the successes and failures in life to achieve it?

In this book, you will learn how to define Purpose, how to identify it, and how to achieve it.

Now, all of this is coming from a relatively ordinary and unassuming guy. I did not create a hot new startup or invent a new technology. I have not starred in movies. I am not a well-known product influencer with millions of followers on TikTok or Instagram. You get the idea. I am a regular guy who started in a corporate job and now sells real estate. But, several years ago, I found my Purpose. My hope is that, precisely because I am a regular guy whose achievements don't necessarily jump off the page, my story will resonate with you. Why? because we *all* are regular people, regardless of the level of success, no matter how big or small.

I did have one major achievement though that was the spark to this fire of Purpose that burns inside me.

A long time ago, I went 10 for 10 in a basketball game, and that performance changed my life, because I realized that the process in it was incredibly instructive. This is not a book about reliving high school sports glory, but rather unpacking how those lessons I learned in sports altered the trajectory of my career.

Everyone deserves to know what their Purpose is. That's how we solve the Purpose problem.

Going 10 for 10 from the foul line changed my life. I know it can change yours as well, so you can find the point in the Purpose!

the warmup
HOW 10 FOR 10 HAPPENED

understanding PURPOSE

PRACTICING FOR THE PRACTICE

Rockland, Maine, is a small mid-coast town (about 9,000 people when I was growing up). While it has evolved into a tourist destination in the summer, its roots are as a true working fishing town. The lighthouse at the end of the mile-long breakwater pridefully protects the harbor, guarding the fishing boats for the lobstermen, which in my opinion is one of the hardest jobs on the planet.

Like many small towns, the locals have a ton of pride in their local sports. While football Friday nights were mandatory in the fall, drawing large crowds, basketball was also a big deal. It gave the town something to cheer for during the long winter months when the sun goes down at 4:30 in the afternoon.

I participated in sports year round—cross country in the fall, basketball in the winter and track in the spring—but basketball was my favorite by far. I loved the game and had played in elementary and junior high. I was always at practice and looked forward to it every day. As a freshman, I watched the junior varsity and varsity teams play and hoped I would have a chance to play on those teams.

By my junior year, I was eligible to be on the varsity team, but that meant nothing. I still had to participate in three days of open tryouts. Everyone assumed who the starting five and main bench players would be, meaning there really were only a few open spots on varsity. I felt like I had a pretty good chance, until I walked into the gym that first day of tryouts. It seemed like there were thirty to forty kids trying out! The math was bad. Almost half wouldn't make varsity *or* junior varsity.

I felt a little better after that first practice, because the coaches for most of that practice did very few drills with basketballs and it was all running. Full court sprints and suicides—running to the foul line and back to the baseline—then running to half court—back to the base line—then running to the other foul line and back to the baseline, *then* finally running the full length of baseline to baseline. If that sounds exhausting, *it is*.

Then after that there was a cage drill which is a flow of players weaving on and off the court playing offense and defense continuously. It's a pretty cool drill to watch, actually. But the drill can last for 15 minutes or more and, again, it's all running. By the end of the day, you were tired, especially if this was your first tryout.

The second day was more of the same, but the group was smaller, as a few just didn't show up, and by the third day it was clear that the players out there were going to all be on one of the teams, and I knew I would *at least* be on JV. I learned that *just showing up* had some benefit!

After tryouts on that third day, the coaches had to set their rosters. Again, it was obvious who would be on the varsity team, and as much as I loved to play, I knew I was not going to be one of those starters. I wasn't the biggest, and didn't have the shooting ability like the rest. But I could run, and I knew the plays, and I could keep up.

Coach called my best friend and me into his office. We were both similar in skills and spent a ton of time together at practice and in school. Coach simply said "Thanks for your hard work at practice. I can tell you that being on the junior varsity team will allow you to play a lot and probably start many games. However, if you want to be on the varsity team, you can be the last two on the roster (which was twelve). You will probably never play. But you will practice with the best. I will let you take the night, and you can tell me your choice tomorrow."

We both looked at each other immediately and told Coach, "I don't need to take the night Coach. I want to play varsity!"

Coach was right. I never did play any significant minutes as a junior, but I did get to play some in my senior year. The practice was starting to pay off.

Coach always taught us that we may not be the best athletes, but we were going to be the best at some things. Two stood out to me.

First off, we would be well-conditioned to run the court and gain control of every loose ball. In turn, we ran *a lot* of suicides. We were not going be tired at the end of the game, and we ran A LOT more suicides. To mix it up, we would just run wind sprints and be timed as a team. If we failed to meet the time, we had to do it again. Make a mistake on a drill, the entire team would have to go to the line. Wind sprints were not as technical as a suicide as you just sprinted from one base line down to the end of court and back. But they were fast and seemingly endless.

We did a ton of loose ball drills, where every loose ball had to be recovered by us. Those drills were amongst my favorite because I always had a chance to compete, like in a real game! That drill had two of us players under the basket back-to-back. Coach would roll the ball out behind us randomly so that we didn't exactly know where it was, then blow the whistle. We would both immediately turn and dive for the ball to gain control. Yes, that screeching sound is your skin sliding on the court! Whoever got control would try to score for the moral victory. Those drills got heated and definitely caused some tense moments, especially when one of the backup bench players would win. I loved those drills, and we all knew if there was a loose ball in a game, we were going to get it.

The second and most important is that we would make our free throws. Not some, but all free throws. Every day after practice, which ended at 9 p.m, practice concluded with free throws. And the drill was very simple. You were allowed to go home when you made 10 free throw shots—all in a row. That meant if you got to the fifth shot and missed, you had to start all over from one.

Think about that for a moment. If you have a basketball, just pick it up and envision what that feels like taking 10 free throws at night at practice. Even in the NBA, the best players in the world fail to make 10 free throws in a row. It was not an easy drill.

As a result, we built an incredible amount of team chemistry, because we were all focused on perfection. We would get to school early and practice free throws. We would wolf down a sandwich at lunch and go to the gym to practice free throws. Study hall? Get your work done and go to the gym and practice free throws. As a result, one night one pure shooter on the team made over 100 in a row! We were not practicing for the game. We were practicing for the practice.

SMALL TOWN BASKETBALL

Houlton, Maine, is not a small coastal town, it's a small border town. With a population of less than 6,000 people today, when you look at it on the map you would think it would just be known for the "end point" of I-95 as it terminates when you cross over into New Brunswick, Canada. But in 1986, it was known as way more than that. They were one of the best high school teams in Maine. Most of us had never even been to Houlton, and all we knew is that they were fast and had a lead scorer that could run circles around most anyone.

Houlton was some 180 miles away, but it appeared as that season went along, Rockland was on a collision course to meet them in the Eastern Maine playoffs, held every year in the famed Bangor Auditorium. The high school playoffs were always centered around winter vacation in February, and the state champion would be determined by the winners of the Eastern Maine and Western Maine semifinal matchups.

As a senior, my hard work was paying off and I even got to start a few games. I had a supporting role, running the court, getting loose balls, rebounds, and assists when possible.

Sure enough, after our Rockland District Fighting Tigers won in the quarterfinals against Bucksport Golden Bucks 58-44, we were set to square off against the top-seeded Houlton Shiretowners. (Talk about a quintessential small-town New England nickname!) The Shiretowners had beaten the Medomak Valley Panthers 71-68 in overtime in the Eastern Maine Class B Basketball Semifinals. We were soon on the bus with the frozen windows driving up the coast on a cold February afternoon to play in a game against the top team in the region.

The game was "over" quickly. Our team was *fast* and was dominating the game with fast-paced scoring, and forcing turnovers that resulted in quick points at a pace that had fans from each team in a frenzy of excitement and bewilderment. At halftime, the lead seemed like a sure thing, but in the second half, their leading scorer took control, and our lead began to shrink. Also, as a couple of our key players got into foul trouble, I was forced to play the entire second half—far more of a key role than anticipated in a state tournament game.

We still had a solid lead, and I recall simply doing the things the coach had taught us to do. Run, be scrappy with loose balls, and make free throws. I made a couple of field goals, and was fouled on one attempt. I made the initial free throw, and I canned the second shot as well. My confidence started to grow in the most consequential game of my life.

The game did go back and forth. Houlton tried everything to cut the lead, which they did, but they weren't ready for a left-handed reserve player who had received little-to-no notoriety during the season. Another drive to the basket. I made both free throws.

When I took a charge for an offensive foul, I went to the line again. Our fans went crazy when I made another one.

As the game ended, their team fouled me one more time out of desperation. I made that one too and in the aftermath, I'm sure my teammates had the look of Marty McFly and Dr. Emmit Brown from *Back to the Future* learning that time travel was possible—a mix of shock and elation! With my final shot, I knew I had just helped our team win the semifinal game to make it to the finals. After all the exhausting drills and grueling late-night practices, I finally had a starring role in a game that meant something.

Our team celebrated at half court. The assistant coach, who had worked with me the whole season, came up to me and said "Brent, do you know what you just did? You just went 10 for 10!"

I had scored 20 points in that game, and they put me on the line as I attempted 10 free throws. I made every one as we knocked off Houlton 96-81.

This story, however, does not exactly have an ending that was ripped out of the script from *Hoosiers*. We played Dexter, a physical team that had reached the state semifinals the previous year.

The championship game didn't start until nearly 10:45 at night because of a leaky roof from a winter storm! (Again, only in New England!) The game was back and forth in a low-scoring affair, and on an already late night, it went into five overtimes. When the final buzzer did go off after midnight, we lost in a 63-61 heartbreaker.

On my end, I played sparingly in that game. While I wished I had been more of a contributor in that championship game, I knew that we had made it to the finals because of my contributions in the semis. I loved playing basketball, and I gave *everything* in every practice to be the best I could. And for one game and one night, I did just that. I went 10 for 10!

The lessons from that game continue to shape me.

YOU ARE NOT THE ONLY ONE

Yes, this story is another "small town America" achievement, and while it will never be on the homepage of ESPN, it matters. Why? Because 10 for 10 was how I lived my life back then. It defined me. And it affected others too, who talked about that game for many years after. For all of us, experiences from early in life define you many years later. In this case, 10 for 10 is a way you can live life, and achieve your greater Purpose.

The story of 10 for 10 is not told just to brag about an experience when I was eighteen. Yes, it is the story of another small-town high school sports achievement, but it has to be told, because ultimately 10 for 10 became the point in my Purpose. To my surprise, the 10 for 10 game was talked about in the small town of Rockland for many years. And while moments like that happen across every swath of America, the 10 for 10 game changed me. Thankfully the chatter about that game for years did exist, because without it, I would have dismissed the experience as something that matters. Actually I *tried* to forget it.

Going 10 for 10 was cool, but I found myself burying the story, because if anything it wasn't that cool and I almost felt embarrassed bringing it up because it sounded like I was bragging or holding on to high school glory days. It wasn't like I made the pros or even played in college.

There are many things amazing about high school graduation, but there is something strange about it too. On the one hand, it feels like an eternity to achieve the celebration of getting the diploma, and then you are instantly immersed into a world that slams you into the reality to work hard, make a lot of money, and be happy. As if it's a scientific formula like the Pythagorean theorem.

That's the Purpose of life, especially coming from your parents. Get out of the house. We raised you. Now, go work hard, make a lot of money, and everything will be fine. For me, that worked for a little while, as I followed that path and had a career in restaurants and hospitality that certainly required a lot of hard work, and I made some good money, especially at a young age. I also did a lot of things that made me happy, going to ball games, concerts, etc. But something was missing. I just wasn't sure what my Purpose was.

Over the years, I've discovered that *a lot* of people don't know what their Purpose is. How do I know? Because I have experienced it personally. I have been that person walking into a corporate meeting with my head down, not making eye contact with others, thus lacking confidence. I have walked into a networking group, unsure of how to clearly convince others that I sell real estate. I have been that person that stopped coming to those networking groups because I grew tired due to lack of quick results. I have been that person who started a new job when I was only in the previous one for less than a couple of years. I *thought I was the only one going through this.*

Over time, as I discovered my Purpose, and worked on achieving it so I could be just a regular guy trying to make a living, I saw that others struggle with their Purpose too! I see the behavior above in others first hand, and hear the stories of people all the time who have done all those things, too. Purpose is hard.

It's only going to get harder, given the world we live in is a 50/50 world with extreme splits on left versus right, creating a culture where it seems like there is no longer an opportunity to have friendly banter over opinions and seeking to understand the root of them. It can seem like an, "I'm right, your wrong" world, with little interest in exploring the identities and backgrounds of those who think differently than us. That creates more tension, more frustration and more of an "I'm on my own" society. Hence, a lack of Purpose.

I think that's why you see the word Purpose so often, because everyone is trying to find it. But Purpose just isn't that easy to find. Take, for example, these speakers that use the word Purpose in their presentations and PowerPoints. Whenever I hear them use the word Purpose, or show it on a slide, I perk up, and wonder if they are going to tell the audience what their Purpose is, or how the audience can discover theirs. However, the message is always assumptive, meaning that they just assume you have a Purpose and the word just looks cool on the slide to fill the presentation or the moment. In the end, I feel like something is missing. I spend so much time thinking and talking about Purpose, that if I think something is missing, there's a good chance the audience feels the same way.

There are, of course, those who think they have an understanding of their Purpose. However, many times events reveal that maybe they are still searching for it, too. Take, for example, my number one sports hero, Tom Brady. Being from Maine, it's probably no surprise that I'm a huge fan. Most people would say his Purpose was to throw footballs and win Super Bowls. Easy, right? But when the events of his retirement, unre-tirement, and divorce publicly played out, I wondered whether his Purpose wasn't so obvious, after all. How could a super famous person have a Purpose problem?

Achieving Purpose is complicated. Everyone, even the "famous" people we look up to, experiences the joy, the pain, and the journey of finding it. That's what makes all of us "regular guys" simply trying to make a living and live a life with Purpose. There are always going to be ups and downs in life and, if the foundation of Purpose is solid, the easier it becomes to properly celebrate the positive ones and tackle the down ones. It doesn't matter if you are the celebrated athlete on TV or the guy watching from his couch.

I was once a director of operations for a restaurant chain, and one busy Saturday afternoon, I visited one of my restaurants to see how the operations were running. It was busy, and chaotic, and while not poorly run, it wasn't perfect either. If you know restaurant operations, you know that nothing is perfect. It's just a controlled chaos environment that either you keep in control, or it controls you.

The manager for the evening shift was arriving, and as he was settling in to get ready to take over the operations, I asked him, "What's your Purpose today?" He looked at me with that half confused, half annoyed look. He just responded, "What's...my... Purpose..?" I smiled back and said "Yeah, What's your Purpose?" It was probably a cruel question to ask at the time, but he tried to answer it anyway, stating all of the things he had to get done throughout the night. I replied with something like "Those are tasks, but what is your Purpose?"

He looked at me slightly bewildered, as if I had asked him to explain Einstein's theory of relativity. He finally just stated, "I'm going to have to think about that." And I left him alone. Go ahead. Try it sometime. Just go up to a friend or a co-worker and ask, "What's your Purpose today?" You will see many confused looks!

Why is Purpose so hard to grasp? Because Purpose isn't a checkbox or deliverable that we cross off at the end of the day. It's not supposed to be a buzzword. And it's not supposed to be a casual conversation word that fills a sentence. It's also not meant to be an emotional word, which many presenters will do to try to make their point. Sure, your Purpose may cause you to be emotional, but that's when you understand how to use the word Purpose.

Purpose is balance. It's a balancing act of learning how to Define it. It's a balancing act of how to Identify it. And, it's the knowledge of how to Achieve it. When you can Define, Identify, and Achieve, you are acknowledging the art of balance and you are on your way to living your greater Purpose.

PURPOSE
defined

LOVING WHAT YOU DO SO THAT OTHERS FOLLOW

I f you can't define a word, you don't have an understanding of it.

The journey of achieving your greater Purpose means that you are prepared to Define, Identify, and Achieve it, meaning you are prepared for the balancing act ahead. There are a couple of exercises that you can do to recognize that Purpose is an art of balance. Reflect on your past and think about times when you were happy, and life was good. Then look back on your past and think about times that you were unhappy.

Earlier in my career, I was working for a company that I loved. It was a fun job that taught me so many lessons and where I made so many friends too. It was hard work, but I loved it and was able to buy my first home as a result. It was a time when I was in "the zone." It was fulfilling work and I was happy.

I also know a time when I was not happy. I had moved jobs and locations in search of something bigger and knew deep down that I was not where I was supposed to be. Long gone was that first house I had bought and now I was the owner of three houses with a housing market recession looming. It was a time when I was *not* in the zone.

When I compare these two times, there are commonalities. When I was in the zone, I was doing what I loved to do, working hard, and making money. When I was not in the zone, I was working hard and making money, but I was not happy doing it.

That's where people end up in so many cases. Money as an end does not equal happiness. The direct deposit hitting your bank account on the first and third Friday of the month, by itself, does not lead to fulfillment. Quite often, professionals settle for what they are doing, hoping that they will be happy one day, and if not, they will just change jobs and the world will be better. Right?

Wrong. Look at all the people who quit their jobs during the pandemic. The Great Resignation. I met so many people during and after the pandemic who started a new job because they were unhappy with the work environment and had some extra cash to try something new. Those who had a plan were successful, while others went back to their old roles as if it were a scene from the movie Groundhog Day.

Quitting your job may be part of the equation, but it's not supposed to be a knee-jerk reaction- especially if you haven't done the hard work of asking yourself what you are truly looking for out of your job, and life in general. (And- the point of this book is Purpose. Not quitting your job!) Interestingly enough, Groundhog Day teaches just that! Once you get past the humor of the repeated catastrophes of each "day," you realize that one thing is being done better every day, as Phil spent an eternity figuring out how to break the cycle.

That's the balancing act. When you begin to understand the times you were happy and instances you were unhappy, the concept of Purpose being an act of balance makes more sense. But how do you internalize it?

When I left high school, I went to college, like you were supposed to do, and I went to work, like I was supposed to do. Why? Because that's what everyone does. We are taught that as soon as possible, you go to work, work hard, make money and be happy. The ingredients and recipe for success are as straightforward as a brownie recipe. So that's what I did. I earned an assistant manager job at Hooters Restaurants and worked as hard as I could to make money. I had a great time during those early years, and got promoted quickly to General Manager, Area Supervisor, even Divisional Vice President.

Hooters sold mainly draft beer. *A lot of it*. This allowed me to have relationships with the beer companies who had some aggressive marketing budgets to take care of their top accounts. I got to do some very cool things like attend two Super Bowls, multiple concerts, baseball, basketball, hockey games, and college football bowl games—in company suites no less! I even got to go on fishing trips to Key West and Costa Rica, as well as drop the green flag at a NASCAR race. It was an exciting time in my life.

Fortunately, I learned how to define Purpose along the way, even though I didn't know it at the time. It happened at one of the bi-annual company meetings that always had a theme with a blend of broad messages, focused breakout sessions, and updates on goals and results. If you were a general manager or higher in rank, you were eligible to attend, and it was often held at a fun hotel or resort to have meetings and team-building experiences. One year we even got to go on a cruise.

At one of these meetings, our company president addressed us. These meetings tend to have the same message repackaged in different ways, all to motivate the group to produce better results. He took the stage after a representative from Human Resources addressed the group and generated about as much excitement as a call from your cable company. The person next to me even whispered, "What's for lunch?" Out of respect, though, when the president of your company takes the stage, you are on point.

He spoke briefly and he talked about leadership. The term of course, is another word used infinitely. Ask ten people what the definition of leadership is and you will get ten varying answers. On this day though, he said something about leadership that I had not heard, and didn't hear again all throughout my corporate career.

"Leadership is something you *love* to do so much, others will simply want to follow you," he said. What? No planning? No Delegation? No Follow up? How could this be leadership? There must be a catch or something coming like SMART goals or habits, or something more. There wasn't. Just that Leadership is something you love to do so much, others will simply want to follow. I wrote that down, and turned my focus back to what was for lunch.

Meanwhile, my career at Hooters was awesome. I grew up with that company, moved several times and got promoted to positions like General Manager, Area Supervisor, and, as mentioned earlier, Divisional Vice President. I was young, and thought I knew what I was doing. However, there was a great deal that I still had to learn.

I did what I thought the position was supposed to do. At such a young age, I had talent to get results. It's one thing to drive results on your own or with a relatively small team. It's another game altogether monitoring several teams in several different states, all with their own individual challenges, and expecting the same overall results. I was now responsible for *inspiring* teams to drive results and had little direct control over them. Given that I was the new guy and responsible for a bulk of underperforming restaurants, combined with my own naivete on the true understanding of the new position, I was definitely swimming in the deep end of the pool.

A few months into the position, the president of the company, and now my boss, the same one who addressed the group and talked about leadership, came into my office one morning and said, "Let's go to lunch." Now, there were two other Divisional Vice Presidents and on this day, we were all in town. Many days we would all go to lunch together, sometimes with other department heads. Today, however, the President asked me and only me. The awkwardness settled in and only grew when the other two started teasing me with a look of, *Well it's been nice knowing you.*

We went to an old restaurant not far from the office that supposedly was famous for its burgers. From what I remember it was a hole in the wall, next to a gas station. We ordered our sandwiches and talked small talk, but it was generally quiet. Bring on the awkwardness.

Your mind dances around in a situation like this, wondering if this is going to be a coaching conversation, or maybe a promotion? No, it couldn't be that. I was too new to the job. Fired? It couldn't be that. Why waste lunch over that? Maybe it was just... lunch.

It was worse. As we finished up and he was paying the bill, he said, "You know, Brent, I know you are relatively new to this job, but if I have to explain to you how to do your job, then I may as well just do your job. And if I do your job, why do I need you?"

Talk about a bombshell. Basically, I was on a short leash. Or was I? When I got back to the office, my two other co-workers wanted to know. "So? What did he say?" they asked. I told them what we discussed, and they simply said again, "It was nice knowing you!" The rest of the day was ruined.

I had to decide how to move forward from there, so that I would be successful in the position, create good results, and learn how to do the job. As I reflect on this part of my life, I realize that I had succeeded based on that one day at a general manager conference when the president talked about leadership. Love what you do so much, that others will simply want to follow! I loved my job and the opportunity, and as a result, there were so many people that wanted to see me succeed and help me with ideas, communication, and relationships.

To achieve your greater Purpose, you must first Define it. Then, you must Identify it, and you have to understand how to Achieve it. Defining your Purpose is indeed that first step. You must LOVE what you do so much, that others will simply want to participate, or follow what you're doing.

READ THE INSTRUCTION MANUAL

Each individual may have their own unique definition of Purpose. Whatever it is, though, the key is that you have a clear definition in place, and embrace the time needed to memorize the definition, as your Purpose will always be the foundation of your core identity. Put another way, it's the instruction manual to assemble your Purpose. *Do not rush this process!*

Rushing this process without a clear definition can lead to a Purpose that has flaws. As a child, I clearly remember Christmas mornings, where my brother tore into his gifts and would just start putting things together, throwing the box aside clearly stating "some assembly required." Inevitably, with the directions nowhere to be found, Christmas cookie sugar high in full gear, on cue he would scream, "Where are the directions?" Undoubtedly, the gift was not assembled properly.

Even if you don't rush the process, you may have to go back and tweak it because you may have overlooked something. IKEA, which probably is Swedish for *one million pieces*, comes with a ton of directions. But even as you sit on the floor for five *#%& hours putting together that beautiful looking desk, somehow one of the drawers doesn't fit right. As you sit there on the floor with an extra washer in hand, you realize that you missed this step a while back and now have to unpack a few steps to correct it! Even when you have the directions, it doesn't mean you will follow them properly.

I've seen this process rushed at work too. Currently, in my role as a managing broker at a small real estate company, I see a lot of newly licensed agents who rush the process to get licensed and affiliated with a brokerage. They are eager to get their business growing and become a mogul like Cliff in *Modern Family*. There is nothing wrong with that, but if you observe their path, many of these new agents are unsuccessful, and either change brokerages multiple times, or leave the business altogether. Why? They didn't take the *time* to define their Purpose of *how* they wanted to grow their business. *They didn't read their instruction manual.*

Real estate brokerages are very different in nature. Some are giant, nationally known names like Coldwell Banker, Remax, Keller Williams, with franchisees that pay for the name and rely on that name to build big teams, spend thousands and thousands of dollars to buy leads and create transactions. Being on one of those teams can generate revenue quickly, and an agent can make some money right out of the gate, with a small percentage split among the larger team. There are a lot of moving parts on these bigger teams, and the environment is fast paced.

Others are small and independent. Unlike at bigger firms, there are no generated leads provided. The agent is in charge of building their own network of prospects. There may or may not be teams, as you do everything yourself, from finding the aforementioned leads to doing all of the administrative work. It can be a slower climb to success. With that in mind, you can end up making more money in the long run as you build your client base, because you are not splitting it several ways with a team—the proceeds are solely yours.

This is the biggest mistake made by real estate agents when they get newly licensed. Unfortunately they didn't have a mentor at that time of choosing a brokerage who asked "How do you want to make a living in this industry?" If you need to make money *now*, and you like structure, team environments, and need constant direction so you can build habits, a bigger firm may be your best path. But if you are self-driven, have good business habits, and have some savings to invest in growing your book of business that produces income and lifestyle, the smaller, independent firm may be the better option.

There is *nothing wrong* with either of these business formulas. But if you don't take the time to define your Purpose, and how you like to work and drive results, and choose the wrong brokerage style, you will fail. It doesn't mean you won't gain clients, but the process may not match your style of how you like to work. In other words, you might make some money, but you won't necessarily be fulfilled. And if that's the case, then what's the point?

Early in my career, I was able to define my Purpose, but I struggled with living it out. Have you ever learned something, but the learning moment was delayed in time? That's what understanding how to define Purpose was for me. I didn't know it at the time because I was caught up in my career, trying to work hard, make money, and be happy. That's how defining Purpose happened for me. It was a delayed learning process that took years. I was using the concept of loving what I do so much others want to follow. The problem was that I wasn't happy. And I knew why. I didn't love what I was doing. I was getting results, but this was only going to be a short-term thing. It could *only* be a short term thing, because I was not growing. Perhaps those who worked for me were growing, but I wasn't growing, and that meant the people I worked for were not growing either. I was not achieving my greater Purpose, and I wasn't sure if I ever would find it.

As a result, I went from doing the same job for fourteen years to suddenly three jobs in four years. And while the companies had changed, my basic role was more or less the same, and I wasn't happy. It really doesn't matter what name is on the marquee of the company. My list of employers included Hooters, Arby's, Margaritas (a regional Mexican chain), and Smokey Bones. All of these restaurant chains had Visions, Missions, Core Values, and KPI's (Key Performance Indicators), just like any other company. I took great pride in learning the "language" of each company so that I could be the best brand ambassador of the company I was working for. Each time I transitioned to another brand, I would do the same thing to learn the organizational ethos and teach it to others to drive results, which I did.

But something was still missing: that damn Purpose. In my early years working for Hooters, I had the best mentors, the best culture, and the best team of peers. It was ingrained in me that leadership was "loving something so much that others wanted to follow." I assumed I would find that with other companies, but it was not the same. It didn't matter what name was on the sign, what state I lived in, or who signed the paycheck. I always ended up in the same place, with no Purpose. I needed something, someone, or some event to help me break the cycle.

Until then, I needed to get out my instruction manual and read it again.

PURPOSE
identified

A LITTLE HELP FROM MAN'S BEST FRIEND

I needed a friend and fortunately I had one—man's best friend. Bronson. Bronson was a Weimaraner, a grey, short-haired dog with longer ears that flopped down the side of their face. Proud in nature, they have a pointer look, and if you see one you notice they stand out in a crowd with their commanding presence.

The day I picked Bronson out of the litter, the breeder told me as I walked up to the litter of several dogs "just be still and watch them. Do not pick the dog. The dog will pick you. When it does, pick it up and put it into the litter. If it comes back to you, you're it." So, I did just that, and after a few minutes, this small grey puppy crawled over my way. It didn't walk back, so I picked it up, held it for a moment, then put it back in the middle of the litter. It immediately came back to me! OK I figured that there had to be at least one other dog that would come my way. I put the dog back in the litter, thinking another one would show interest. Nope. The same dog just came straight back to me. I picked up the dog, and walked over to the breeder and said, "I guess we got a dog".

The breeder looked at me and said, "This is a male. There were only two males in the litter. Are you sure it picked you?" I looked at her curiously and said "Yes, it picked me three times". She questioned me and said, "Have you ever had a male Weim? Have you ever even had a Weim for that matter?" "No, does it matter having a male vs. female?" The breeder shrugged with a look that all but said, "good luck ...."

Weimaraners tend to be stubborn, and I was in over my head as Bronson was a handful. Have you ever seen or read *Marley & Me*, featuring the world's worst dog? Bronson was in the running. He never chewed furniture, but he would do things like eat toilet paper-the whole roll. But it was a game. He would pull the paper from the bathroom hall and unroll it into the living room, like fifteen to twenty feet! At other times, he would somehow pull out a CD from the sound system rack and destroy the cover. Not the regular plastic covers, but the ones that had cardboard special cases. He would shred them. Just to let you know he was there when you weren't.

Wherever I went, so did Bronson. *Everywhere.* If I went upstairs, he went upstairs. If I went to the basement, so did he. If I went to the bathroom, he wanted in there too. If I went to the garage and closed the door, he would wait on the other side of the door till I came back. One time there was a leak in the kitchen sink, and I had to crawl under to fix it. Guess who also insisted on crawling in there? Bronson.

Most things were a game to Bronson, but his favorite game was Frisbee. Over the years we had several frisbees, but his favorite was one of those pink floppy frisbees with a stitched rubber outside that was easy to throw. The game was his favorite and he was the best at it! The laser focus of his eyes, along with his front leg positioned like a track star before the start of an olympic event let you know nothing else mattered but catching that frisbee, daring me to throw it at any distance. And when I did throw it, he would *always* catch it, and would *always* bring it back so I could throw it again.

This actually was more than a game for Bronson. It was his life. Except that once he engaged you in the game, it was game over-or game on, if you will! When he sucked you into his world, you were committed to the game. With all the energy Bronson had, he demanded an hour or two a day to be "in the game!"

How would he do this? Bronson was clever. Many times, he would just come up to me and put his head in my lap. It would seem affectionate. Then I would pet him, and he would somehow have had the frisbee on the floor nearby, and in one motion would leave my lap, pick up the frisbee, and then *jam* the frisbee in my lap! If I touched the frisbee and tossed it to the floor, the game had begun.

Then there were the times when I was in the game when I really didn't want to be in the game. One game was called Mow the Lawn. I would mow the lawn, and Bronson would bark until I let him outside. He had a couple methods of playing the game. One would be that as I was on a line, he would dart up and toss the frisbee in front of the lawnmower in the tall grass. I had to stop, which meant the mower would shut off, walk up to grab the frisbee, and throw it. It was on. The next pass or two, he would have the frisbee in his mouth, and as I was making the turn for the next pass, he would stand on the line ahead and take a giant crap! Now I was forced to stop, pick up his shit, and walk back to the mower, in which the frisbee was next to it now. And of course when I tossed it aside, you know the rest of the story. I was in the game.

I tried hiding the frisbee, but he would always find it. *Always.* He was so good at frisbee you could throw it at night in the woods, and he would find it. You could put the frisbee inside, but he would just find a rock to take the place. I didn't want him chewing on rocks, so the solution was something softer, like... a... frisbee... *You were in the game.*

No one was exempt from the game. The only way to avoid the game was to not opt in. The only way to do that was to not engage with Bronson's tactics, which included petting him on the head. One summer afternoon, I had a friend and his female date on the back deck with some beverages. The female friend was dressed nicely in all-white clothes. After we'd been sitting at the table for a few minutes, Bronson came over to her and put his head on her chair. She said "Aw, how cute" and petted him.

Game on.

He subsequently went to fetch his frisbee and lightly nudged her chair. She took the frisbee and tossed it over the deck.

Now, the deck was about fifteen feet above the ground, so Bronson had to run down the stairs, which he would do countless times a day. But, since it was summer, you can imagine the red-dirt Georgia clay that was caked on the frisbee as he brought it back. Bronson brought the frisbee upstairs to play again. She chose to be out of the game. Bronson didn't care and jammed the slobbery, clay-covered frisbee right behind her lower back into the chair! As she stood up in a mix of horror and frustration, the entire back side of her summer white clothes were now wet with red clay, spritzed with dog slobber. Clearly upset, she went inside to allegedly use the restroom. After checking on her a few minutes later, she was gone and we never saw her again. Bronson had ruined the afternoon date, and didn't seem to care because the game was back on.

Bronson didn't care where we lived, as long as the game could be played. For me, my favorite place was on the beach. For a couple of years, I lived in Destin, Florida, and we were within walking distance to the Gulf. (You're not allowed to say *ocean* there). Winter was the best time to live there, because in those days the town really slowed down as the summer tourists were gone and you could actually drive around the area without budgeting an hour to get from one side of town to the other. That meant that the beaches were wide open too, and there was nothing like a grey ghost dog sprinting through the white sand to gracefully catch a perfectly thrown frisbee.

Bronson was so excited on those mornings going to the beach that he knew exactly where to go and which ramp to the beach we would take. He would sprint from the house over to the ramp and down to the beach, and just sat there until I caught up. He knew I would be there for him, and he would wait, ready to play the game.

Despite his insistence on playing the game, he was the most patient friend you could have. The days of shredding cardboard CD cases were long gone, and I could leave him alone in the house all day while I was at work. During that part of my career I worked a lot, many of which were upwards of twelve hours per day. My career had resulted in a move, this time to Connecticut, where I had a small house in North Haven. The house was modest, but it had a really nice level and large backyard which was fenced. I didn't care that the kitchen was an old galley kitchen that wasn't updated, or that the rooms were small. When I saw that yard, I knew it was a perfect house, because Bronson would have a great place to catch the frisbee!

This house had a nice bay window with a ledge in the living room, and the way it laid out, the couch was in front of the bay window looking to the only appropriate wall to set up the TV. It seemed to work out for what it was. It was a nice bay window with crank out windows that would let in lots of light and fresh air, with a ledge that you could put plants, decorations on, etc.

Not long after I moved there, and started working, I learned about Bronson's patience. As I drove down the road toward the house, I saw something odd in that bay window that didn't look right. As I pulled into the driveway though, it looked perfect. Bronson had decided that the ledge of the bay window was the perfect place to wait for me till I came home, and he was lying on the ledge! As I pulled in, he lifted his head with excitement. I was home and you know what that meant—time for the game!

As work ground on, I began to wonder if this was all I was supposed to do. Working day after day, shift after shift in the restaurant industry had become less satisfying, and while I was good at what I did, I enjoyed it less and less. I couldn't see myself doing this forever, but I didn't know how to change what I was doing. I certainly didn't want to give up the money! I guess I just needed to work hard, make more money, and somehow that would make me happier.

But I wasn't happy, and I found myself asking more frequently, "What is my Purpose?" What am I supposed to do? The answer was always the same—get your ass ready for work. At least Bronson would be waiting for me when I got home.

Summer in New England is beautiful and my house in North Haven was no exception. Perfect weather, combined with the grill fired up ready for a steak, music on the back deck, and a cold beverage makes for the perfect day!

You know who else loved these perfect days? Bronson! If I was home on the back deck, that meant there was going to be a lot of time for him to play frisbee. A perfect day! Now, over the years of his life of nearly fourteen years, I figured that I probably threw the frisbee to him around 10,000 times. A classic act of throwing the frisbee, catching the frisbee, returning the frisbee, and repeat.

As this Sunday afternoon wore on and the sun began to set, I started thinking again about what my Purpose was, knowing that the next day I would be right back at work. I was beginning to think that my Purpose was to just work in the same field forever, and whenever this job ended, I would find another.

But something happened that Sunday afternoon that was an *aha* moment I will never forget, the kind of moment that makes you freeze with goosebumps, even on a warm summer evening. I was throwing the frisbee and Bronson was catching it. Then it hit me.

Bronson's Purpose was to catch the frisbee. My Purpose was to simply throw it! It was simple. I throw the frisbee and Bronson catches it. As I froze and thought about it, Bronson waited for me to process it.

Holy Shit! Could it be that simple? Bronson can't

catch the frisbee unless I throw it. And I can't throw the frisbee if Bronson doesn't bring it back to me.

I had just identified what Purpose was.

By identifying my Purpose, which in this case was throwing the frisbee, I acknowledged that I was helping someone else achieve their Purpose too, which in Bronson's case was catching the frisbee. Purpose isn't what you do, it's who you are. Purpose isn't an act of selfishness. It's the act of knowing who you are so you can help someone else know who they are. In this case it took a dog to teach me that–and several thousand frisbee tosses.

I didn't realize it at the time, but I was now smack in the middle of truly understanding the balance of Purpose. My corporate career had taught me how to Define Purpose, and my dog had taught me how to Identify Purpose. But as I drove up the highway that next day to work, it would be years before I put the two together, for my time to put it all together and achieve it was still several years away.

Work hard, make money, and be happy. Right?

THE MERGING OF PASSION AND PURPOSE

Many people cringe at the thought of speaking in public, whether it's giving a talk, presentation, or answering questions. Glossophobia is the technical term for a strong fear of public speaking, and upwards of 75% of humans have it to some degree. Public speaking is in fact the number-one fear in America—more so than even death! As Jerry Seinfeld eloquently put it, "To the average person, if you go to a funeral, you're better off in the casket than giving the eulogy."

I, however, love speaking in public. I have always felt comfortable speaking in front of groups and the larger the group, the more of a high I get. It's not that I like having the spotlight on me; it's about presenting thoughts and ideas to a group of people and watching them listen to the message. The better the message, the more intently they listen, and I have always strived to make sure that the message is good, so the audience doesn't feel as if they have wasted their time.

It's no different than going to church and listening to the preacher talk. Sometimes you feel the connection that the preacher is talking *directly* to you! Other times, you are bored and can't wait to get out of there. Why? Because you feel like you have wasted your time.

Going to the bar for a drink is similar too. The best bartenders make an effort to know your name, remember your favorite beverage, engage in conversation, and make knowledgeable suggestions when you are unsure of what you want. When this happens, customers don't want to leave and end up ordering a second or third round. There are also the bad bartenders. They could not give two shits that you are there, barely know the menu, and avoid eye contact.

But they still expect a tip. You can't wait to get out of there because you have wasted your time.

Interestingly, public speaking, church, and a bar all relate to each other. In each one, there is a crowd of people on one side of the audience, expecting to be served. Separated only by a stage, a podium, or a bar, the other party is ready to serve.

What side of the bar do you prefer to be on?

You won't see me on Sundays preaching but I'm happy to step behind the bar and pour you a shot. Of Purpose of course! And I won't waste your time.

After the "frisbee" moment that summer with Bronson, which taught me how to identify Purpose, I began to think about the work/money/happiness balance in a different way. What if you chose to be happy, doing what you loved to do, put in the hard work by working your ass off, and had faith that the money would come? Could that be possible? I wasn't so sure, because that meant something would have to change, namely me. And as the falling of the Oak leaves crushed the hopes and dreams of those summer nights on the deck with Bronson and his frisbee, I was overcome with a story I learned in a much warmer place, Miami.

THE LADDER

Many years ago, I was enrolled in an Audio Video production school located in South Beach Miami. My teacher, who's name I can't remember, taught me something that I will never forget that sums up the art of Promise Perfectly. The *ladder.*

Picture yourself in a room, and the only way out is to climb a ladder to the top of the ceiling and open a hatch that allows you to get to the top, and "escape" if you will. It's a tall room, maybe 20 feet tall. You look around and eventually find a ladder! As you stand on the ladder up to the top you realize the importance of the simple rungs, because they assist you, one step at a time to climb to the top, something you could *never* do in just one large step. Along each rung, or step you gain "key" experiences, all producing small souvenirs that you put in your pocket. Every rung, a new Key. A new experience. A new souvenir. Your pockets begin to fill up, and overflow, and you are carrying these things with you, an accumulation of souvenirs on the entire journey upward.

Finally, you reach the top of the ladder! You can see the light through the hatch! You push up on the hatch and... it won't open. Frustrated, you look closer at the situation and you are staring at a simple padlock that is holding the latch locked. You need a key to unlock it.

Now what? As you stand on that top rung, legs getting tired, you think about all of the rungs you have climbed. And you realize, early on, you had previously found the *key!* It was a small key and you put it in your pocket. All you have to do is dig into the pocket and grab the key, hold the lock with one hand and open the lock with the other hand. Success is imminent. There is one problem, though. In order to do this, you have to drop something. You must pull something out of the pocket that you think is important and drop it, because you can't hold everything. It's important because you may need it for something else or you just want to hold on because you can't picture life without it. But all you have to do is drop it and let it go so you can get the key and open the hatch.

What happens next is the difference between working hard, making money, and being happy, versus being happy, working hard and having the faith the money will come.

All you have to do is make that *sacrifice* and you can move on. If you don't make that sacrifice, you can't open the hatch. You run out of strength and have to go back down the ladder to maybe find another way, only to learn that at some point you have to climb the ladder *again*, and you are going to have to let that one thing go.

And you know what the most screwed up part of the sacrifice (the thing you have to let go) is?

You already know what it is and it scares the living shit out of you.

Not only does letting that one thing go scare you, you know once you climb out of the hatch and close the door, it's locked again, and it *won't reopen.* You are making a decision that's permanent.

I climbed that damn ladder a ton of times! I realized that I had the key the whole time, which was having the mindset to *be happy and do what I loved,* which was selling real estate and speaking to groups about Purpose. I would have to work hard to create a network of people who believed in me to help them with their real estate goals, as well as receive speaking invitations. I wasn't worried about any of that.

I was worried, however, about how to make any money and financially support myself. The guaranteed paycheck was the item I had to drop. I was afraid of how to make the money doing something I wanted to do but didn't know how to do.

How do you flip the script for good and choose to be happy, work hard, and make money? For me I had to leave the job with a biweekly check. The notion scared the hell out of me, but once I became comfortable with that, there was no going back.

Disclaimer: Again, this is not a book to tell you to quit your job! Perhaps you are up for a huge promotion, but you will have to move your family. Maybe you just started a new job and you are nervous because the technology and culture is drastically different from previous experiences. It could be the new home you are buying for your family is more expensive and you may not be able to travel as much or go out to eat as much as you are used to.

Whatever the goal is on top of that roof, you know you have to have the key to open it. And while you are hesitant to let that one big thing go, remember: The bigger the reward, the bigger the sacrifice can be. And having to let something *big* go, it scares the hell out of you. The bigger the reward, the bigger the sacrifice can be.

TELL ME SOMETHING YOU WERE PROUD OF

Suddenly, I was at a crossroads. I knew how to define Purpose, from my leadership experiences at work. I knew how to identify it, thanks to Bronson, whom I never stopped throwing the frisbee to, even as he aged, albeit at shorter distances. But I still didn't know how to achieve it. Actually, I was achieving it, but I couldn't put it into context. In the end, my experience as a high school basketball player helped me achieve it, and it has formed the foundation of the framework that I strongly believe in. I just didn't know it until I was forced to resurrect the memory.

The memory, brought back to life, was the result of a lunch that I had with a very successful keynote speaker and entrepreneur who has started many successful businesses. He did me a favor by speaking at a Marietta Business Association luncheon. I had expressed interest in public speaking, and he graciously accepted an invite to lunch one day.

About midway through the lunch, he asked me "Tell me something you were proud of." I quickly responded that I was proud that I had a broker license that would help me in my career. He said that's great, but I know thousands of brokers and they all talk about real estate.

That almost sounds boring. "Tell me something you were proud of that many people don't know about."

I sat there for what seemed like an eternity. An otherwise noisy restaurant suddenly seemed like a library. I thought back as far as I could go and with a sense of embarrassment I said, "Well, I went 10 for 10 once in an important basketball game, and it was probably my greatest achievement that I remember to this day. I just don't talk about it much."

He replied, "What is 10 for 10?" So, I briefly told him the story.

"I would listen to *THAT.*"

Holy shit. I remember driving home in silence. I started thinking about the story of 10 for 10. When I got home, I began to revisit the whole story from high school and dug it back out. And as I continued exploring all of my memories and experiences, I began to solve the *equation,* if you will, of Purpose.

At the same time, I began to understand why the Purpose problem can be so hard to solve, and why something in principle should be simple but in reality is very difficult to do. I think the reason for that is because as humans we want things to be simple. On its face, Purpose is simple. Everything has a Purpose, or a job, and that is easy enough to understand.

Take, for example, an airplane propeller. Its Purpose is pretty damn simple. Rotate. When it does its job properly, the plane flies. If the propeller *doesn't* rotate, bad shit is about to happen.

But for us humans, the Purpose *isn't* that simple. There is way more to it, because humans experience joy and happiness, as well as sadness, anger, and fear. Things, meanwhile, have no emotion and don't care. Humans, however, do. That's why Purpose becomes vague, and why most people question their Purpose, or don't even have one. To be clear, everyone will experience those highs and lows in life *regardless* if they know what their Purpose is, or not. But if you *know* what your Purpose is, you will know how to *build* on the highs to keep them going and get even better results in your life, and you will know how to *adapt* off the lows in your life to create new momentum.

And so, my reader, let's pour a drink so you can ponder over the three steps of having Purpose, for *you*. And remember, it's not going to be about just working hard, making money, and being happy. It's about *you* becoming fulfilled and doing what you truly love to do, which will naturally create hard work, resulting in the faith that the money will come.

1. You have to be able to *Define* your Purpose. I did that through my corporate job. I learned that leadership is loving what you do so much that others will want to participate. It's important to take time to reflect on that and think about if what you are doing is something you love to do. If the answer is yes, great. If the answer is no, what is it that you *love* to do?

2. You have to be able to *Identify* your Purpose. I did that through the help of Bronson, remember? I learned that in order to achieve my Purpose I had to be helping someone else achieve theirs too, which in this case was throwing a frisbee so a dog could catch it, which was his Purpose. Are you doing things that you love to do *and* that have actions that help others? If not, maybe you should think about who you are throwing the frisbee to.

3. You have to *achieve* your Purpose. That's where 10 for 10 comes in! I remember! I did it once before, why not again? What if you just applied the basic principles of making a free throw to your life as you live it? I realized not only was it possible, but I had been doing it my whole life.

Purpose is your *life*. 10 for 10 is how you *live* your life.

PURPOSE
achieved

HOW 10 FOR 10 WORKS

I spent months thinking about 10 for 10. The Game. The Practice of shot after shot. The Promise I had to make to myself to stay focused. The Accomplishment of getting to play and make an impact for my team.

I am a "yellow pad" guy, and that's how I take notes. I have to write it down. I can't take screenshots, do voice memos, scan things, etc. If I want to see it, memorize it, think about it, I *have* to write it down, and the yellow pad is my go to. As I reviewed page after page of notes, the rules of 10 for 10 began to surface, and I realized that if 10 for 10 was going to mean anything, that every shot should have a name. That actually was easy, because the equation of Purpose was solved. 10 for 10 is how you achieve your Purpose, and each shot represents a moment in my life. I had already taken these shots but just didn't know they existed.

Purpose is, in fact, your life. 10 for 10 is how you live it. And just like anything you do, there is a process. The same is true for 10 for 10. Let's look at the process:

Every shot has a name associated with it, and the names mirror a point in your life.

Some of the names are more obvious than others, but the process needs to be simple to understand so you can embrace what you are about to experience.

The goal is to make 10 in a row. If you miss, you go back to the beginning, regardless of what shot you are on.

Life experiences of achieving your greater Purpose are going to have all sorts of emotions. I thought of the countless times I made or missed shots, and experienced highs and lows of my career and life. I kept tying it back to those times I would take actual shots in practice, and lined them up with my experiences.

You will have a specific emotion with every shot you take, and it intensifies as you progress, or regress. The emotion will change and become more intense as you attempt all 10 shots, because in life, just as at the foul line, there is both anticipation and anxiety that comes with the opportunity of making, but also missing, the shot.

We all have a "sixth sense" if you will, and these emotions of anticipation and anxiety tie in with your feelings, meaning, you kind of know the result already. If something is going to be great, you feel it, like proposing to your girlfriend. You got a pretty good idea she will say Yes! If something is going to be wrong, you feel that too, like if your job is going to be eliminated. If you feel something is good, or something is bad, you are probably right.

I had written down all of the shots, given them names, thought about the stories I could tell, and the tales I have listened to from friends, colleagues, even strangers. I began to realize that *everyone* could go 10 for 10 and if they embraced the concept, they could find and achieve their Purpose too. I have stated many times: *I don't think people know what their Purpose really is.* Maybe that's because we struggle to learn from our experiences.

Every shot has a lesson.

I will explain in detail later, but these shots have either one of three lessons: Promise, Practice, or Accomplishment. Once I tied it back to those high school experiences, I was able to unlock them so that I had a laser-focused mindset on how each shot worked and progressed with each attempt resulting in the made, or missed, shot. In basketball, the free throw can be so beautiful as it swishes through the net, with the whisper and snap as the ball glides through perfectly. It also can be incredibly ugly as it clangs off the rim so everyone instantly knows it's a miss. Regardless of the make or miss, there *still* is a lesson to be learned.

Then the most important part of the process. Picture yourself on the line, holding a basketball, the clock is stopped, and there you are on the line getting to take the shot.

All. By. Yourself.

Only YOU can take the shot.

You can't give the shot to someone else! You have to take it and own the results. Make it and advance. Miss it and start over. Ask me how I know!

In basketball, free throws are one of the most freeing–and constraining–aspects of the game. It is the one time during the game when a player is completely unguarded. If you miss a free throw, the only person to blame is yourself – not a bad pass by a teammate, not stingy defense by the opposing team, and not a bad call by the referee. And yet, that freedom and ultimate accountability can get into the player's heads.

There have been times where I wanted to take the shot. There were times when I didn't want or even refused to take the shot out of fear of missing or what may happen as a result. But in the end, you can make all of the excuses you want (I certainly did), but the shot is yours to take. Make or Miss, that's the beauty of the game.

There are days I feel confident about the results of my efforts–I know the ball is going through the hoop. Those times included days that I list a house for a client, and with multiple showings and offers submitted. In my line of work, that's a great day! In those times, I know the hard work of getting the listing and marketing the listing will pay off. Let's go.

On other occasions, I've been unsure of my preparation–the release doesn't feel quite right as the ball leaves my hand. On those days, the listing has sat there for three months because the seller wanted to price it too high, and now calls every day inquiring why it isn't selling. New day, same call, no sale, and tomorrow will be the same. Please let someone else take the shot!

But I can't let someone else take the shot. It's on me to take it and be accountable for the results. If the house doesn't sell right away, it's on me to constantly evaluate the marketing of the house, and educate my client that there is a blend of product versus price and when that blend is correct, the house will sell. Give me the ball.

The parallel of taking the shot and accountability crosses into all success and failures. Too often we say *I didn't get that promotion because my boss was an asshole.* Or, *my girlfriend doesn't make me feel fulfilled because of* .... (I will let you fill in the blank, as I don't want to be blamed for giving you any ideas!) You take the credit for the wins. 10 for 10 teaches you to take the credit for the losses.

Using this methodology, only you can take the shot because it's your life and your game of 10 for 10. You are the only one that can take the shots, learn from the misses, as well as grow from the makes and successes.

I spent a lot of time earlier on leadership, but here is more of a light-hearted description that while tongue and cheek, is pretty spot on:

There are Three kinds of leaders that exist:

1. Those who *Make* things happen.
2. Those who *Watch* things happen.
3. Those who say "*What the hell just happened?*"

As funny as that can be, the reality is that we have all been that kind of leader at one point or another! I know I have been all three! There *is* an interesting balance of the first two, because great leaders who make things happen spend a ton of time observing and evaluating, so they can learn what works and what doesn't. They apply those observations to their own style. That said, too much watching, without a lot of action, isn't exactly a recipe for dynamic leadership. Meanwhile the third type—reflexively deflecting blame with no accountability—just becomes an *excuse* over time. You will never go 10 for 10 with this outlook.

The lessons will make more sense as you take each shot.

I admit that at times I wondered if I was overthinking Purpose, and all of the elements, but I was too far down the path of exploring it, questioning it, and perfecting it. That's why I need to explain just a little bit more about the lessons of these shots I am about to describe—a pregame warmup if you will— so you are prepared to make the most out of your own journey, identify your own Purpose, and make that walk to the line for Shot 1.

PROMISE

Promise, like Purpose, is one of those words that get used all of the time, yet has several different layers to the use. How many times do you say the word promise? How many times does your friend, spouse, coworker use the word promise?

Here's the key to Promise. Every promise that you make to someone or someone makes to you involves a sacrifice. It may not be a big sacrifice, but it's still there nonetheless.

Have you ever asked or been asked to pick someone up at the airport? Think about picking someone up at the airport. This situation has inevitably come up, promising to pick a friend or family member up. "What time do you land?" "Friday, about 4:30 pm? Ok. I will be there at about 5pm."

I promise.

The words *I Promise* are now active. I live in Atlanta, so this comes up routinely, but it applies to any other major city with rush hour traffic. The sacrifice of time is in play here, because you now have to plan your afternoon accordingly so that you don't get distracted at work, leaving on schedule to get to the airport in time so your loved one is not waiting on you. If you are on time to pick them up, the conversation on the way home is *much* more pleasant than if you are late. All of a sudden, you are stressed because you are late, and they are stressed because they want to get home.

The sacrifice you make when you say the words *I Promise* is an instant commitment, whether you have thought about that sacrifice or not. That's why Promises get broken, because the sacrifice is not thought about, recognized, or identified when you say the words.

Simple to make, yet hard to keep, are promises that involve your time. Time is the most precious asset, in my opinion, and I *hate* wasting my time, or others.

An example of this is moving day. I moved so many times in my earlier life that while I was good at moving quickly, it *always* was a pain in the ass. And there were times when I had to ask for help. That sucks too, because moving day is typically on a Saturday, which is everyone's day off, and I stress over people giving up their time on a day off to help me.

Same thing goes the other way. Someone has to move and they need help and they know I own a truck. People love those who own trucks come moving day! We all have been there on a Saturday at some point, being helped, or helping others move. It's not that fun, other than some beer and pizza, especially if it's a hot 90 degree day or, worse, 40 degrees and raining! As much as there have been times when I didn't want to spend my Saturday helping a friend, I did, because I made the promise.

What about the guy who *didn't show up* though? Whether I was moving or helping someone else move, when I learned that someone didn't show up after they *promised* to help, it didn't matter the reason. My mind naturally went to a place that challenged the fullness of that person's credibility.

Showing up is half the battle. Even if a guy that was part of moving day wasn't the strongest guy to lift furniture, he still contributed, which was way better than not showing at all.

Promises are progressive! The more sacrifices you make when keeping promises to others, the more your *credibility* grows. The more lies you tell when breaking your promise (face it, it's a lie to *yourself* when you break it) crush your credibility.

When you go 10 for 10, you too will be forced to make promises, and experience those sacrifices first hand.

I Promise.

PRACTICE

The Allen Iverson quote rings true here. *Practice? Who needs Practice? Are we really talking about Practice?*

Yep, we sure are! This is no post-game rant on practice but let's talk about it regardless.

The word practice is self-explanatory in nature, like Purpose and Promise, but unlike those words, which can be overused to make a presentation stimulating, Practice tends to be avoided. Why? Because it revolves around Work. It revolves around Effort. And it revolves around Repetition. Practice is the *story* that no one wants to read, because it's boring. There is nothing attractive or sexy about practice, which is probably why the iconic NBA star didn't want to talk about it either. We, by nature, demand quick fixes so we can move on to the next thing, but it's the long hard and boring work, also known as *Practice,* that validates fulfillment and happiness.

Earlier we learned that your Purpose should bring happiness, loving what you do, buying into hard work, and having the faith that the money will come. It is a lifestyle. This is much different than the mindset we were taught growing up, which was to go to your job, work hard, make money, and be happy—as if it were a simple arithmetic problem. To be great at your work in either one of these scenarios, you must always be practicing your skills so that you are ready to produce high-level results for your work, peers, clients, friends, etc.

Would you rather be *told* what to do, or *inspired* what to do? There is a difference. Practice is not fun when you are told what to do, and especially when you just aren't motivated to put in the practice. When you lose the inspiration, the results will not be there. All results have consequences, which show up in the level of accomplishments you achieve.

As an example, I'll go back to my previous experience in the restaurant industry years ago, where I had the privilege of being a director of operations in both a corporate role and a franchising role for Hooters and Tilted Kilt, respectively.

When you work in a corporate setting, you are responsible for hitting goals, results, KPIs, OKRs, or however your company wants to label them. In a director role, you manage people whom you oversee, and they are held accountable for hitting those goals, both with their people and their financials, while maintaining the brand. If they hit those goals, they are compensated and maybe over time, even get promoted. If they don't hit those goals, they get fired. Essentially, working in that corporate role is telling people what to do.

When you work in a franchising setting, you are responsible for creating and building relationships with the franchisee, who wrote a big check to be able to put a sign on the building and expects that they can just open the doors and print money because of that sign. They may or may not truly understand or love the brand as much as the corporate entity, becoming frustrated with the organization because they are not printing money and must start paying off their loans. In this setting, you can't tell them what to do, because you can't fire them. They don't technically report to you. Their investment in the franchise bought their autonomy. Essentially working in that franchise role is inspiring people what to do.

Practice is not fun when you are told what to do, and especially when you aren't motivated to put in the practice.

However, practice is fun when you are inspired by what to do, because it comes within you. People, (especially us bartenders out there pouring you a drink!) are generally unmanageable. But they *are coachable.*

Nobody likes being told what to do, unless they are first inspired. When you inspire someone they *trust* you, and they want to drive results. If you are inspired by your boss, your spouse etc., you also want to get great results at work and at home. As a result, you don't mind being told what to do at times because of the inspiration.

This made so much more sense to me when I was working in the restaurant industry with franchisees! When a franchisee writes the check for the brand, and consistently pays their royalties on time to the franchisor, my best way to get results with them was to inspire them how to do things better that would ultimately make them more profitable. For sure, I tried the asshole role of threatening compliance and default, but that only put up a wall between them and the brand, which was me. But when I started focusing on the things they were doing right (even if they were few and far between), asked them their concerns and addressed one or two things to solely focus on, the trust began to build because they were inspired. As a result, I was able to effectively tell them what to do now, because they wanted great results in that area too. It's a much better approach to inspire results versus demanding them.

Way back when I was in high school working on my free throws, I just wanted to be on the team. *I was inspired!* So, I was in the role of being told what to do by Coach, which in this case was to perfect the free throws to go 10 for 10, just like every night at the end of practice.

The *last* thing you wanted to do at night was to be on the foul line missing free throws, because that just delayed the inevitable: getting home late, eating late, and doing homework late. It added to the stress and exhaustion of day-to-day life. The earlier you were able to get home, the better.

Not going 10 for 10 at practice had real consequences!

As a result, every time there was a break in the schedule at school, you would always see one of the players in the gym working on their skills. Sometimes it was a play, or a move to the basket, but it *always* included free throws. It may have been before school, sneaking out at lunch or study hall (the cafeteria was right across from the gym), or right after school before the other teams that shared the gym started their practice.

We were not waiting to practice for the game, we were *practicing* for the practice! This taught me something I have worked on my whole life. Vince Lombardi once said, "If you cheat yourself in practice, you'll cheat yourself in a game; and if you cheat in a game, you'll cheat yourself for the rest of your life." This is one of my favorite quotes! If you take practice seriously enough to put in extra time for the practice, it can only help you be even *better* in the game. And the game here is indeed, *your life.*

When you practice for the *practice*, the practice for the *game* will be so much more meaningful. And when you play the *game*, you know that you have done everything you can to play the game as good if not better than anyone else.

In the end, we *all* experience times where we are told what to do. While we would rather be inspired by what to do, if you stay focused on the *Practice,* your efforts of focusing on the process, rather than the outcome, will keep you intrinsically motivated. In the long run, you will be happier, more fulfilled, and more successful because the results, regardless of how you were told/inspired to accomplish them, are all yours.

I Promise.

ACCOMPLISHMENT

You don't have to think too hard to define the word accomplishment. It's something you do that makes you proud of your efforts. It's your reward from all of your hard work. It's important though that you spend the time to recognize these accomplishments, so you can build on them to continue to get improved results and rewards.

There can be some traps, though, with accomplishment. One of those traps is that once we experience accomplishments, we tend to think it will continue, and take for granted the continued success.

I remember the first time I got a bonus check when I worked at Hooters. It was incredible! I didn't expect it, and looked at the check for extra money that I didn't anticipate. Talk about an accomplishment! I was fired up to go to work and continue to work hard to see what the next bonus check could look like. But over time, something happened to me that happens to the best of us. I *expected* that bonus check, and every month one showed up, the incredible feeling began to wear off. No longer was I looking at the extra money with that incredible emotion. Instead, I cashed it and went to work the next day.

You see lots of examples like this in sports. Programs that win the title one year, and are supposed to just reload, only to be knocked off by a hungry upstart. As former women's soccer star Mia Hamm said, "It is more difficult to stay on top than get there."

Sports history is littered with talented teams that expected to be repeat champions, only to fall short when they didn't work as tirelessly the second go-round once they had a taste of success. In keeping with our earlier basketball example, the 2004 Los Angeles Lakers, who had won three consecutive titles from 2000 to 2002, signed Hall of Famers Gary Payton and Karl Malone in the offseason prior to the 2003-04 season, pairing them with superstars Shaquille O'Neal and Kobe Bryant. On paper, arguably no NBA team has had a better collection of talent and experience.

The Lakers' product on the court, however, never measured up to their prodigious talent on paper, in large part because they didn't work enough. Even in the midst of a run to the NBA Finals, chemistry issues were cited all year. That was evident in the NBA Finals, as they went up against the Detroit Pistons, who played tenacious team defense despite not having a true star. The Lakers eventually folded like origami, losing to the Pistons 4-1 in the Finals. On cue, O'Neal was shipped out in the offseason and the Lakers' dynasty crumbled like a cookie that had been left in the oven too long.

What is the takeaway from one of the most successful organizations in professional sports? The key to avoiding this trap is remembering that *there is no greater feeling than receiving that first paycheck in a new job, and there is no worse feeling than receiving your last paycheck once you've been fired from that job.*

I think about this differently now as I think about my job selling real estate. When I work with a client on selling their house and buying a new one, I expect and anticipate that accomplishment of getting my client to *keys* and *cash* day. I know that my hard work to educate my clients, negotiate contracts, follow up on key dates, and monitor any details that could hold up the process will pay off so that ultimately my clients are happy, and of course I get paid too. But when I get paid, *I'm fired.* I have to continue to work hard to find another client so that I can continue to make a living.

So when I get paid, it's like getting the first check *and* last check at the same time. Shit! If only I had taken that approach in my previous jobs!

If you treat every paycheck with the mentality of being excited like it's your first, and cognizant that it could be your last, you can avoid this trap. Even *if* you find yourself where you are experiencing a "last" check from your current job, your mindset puts you in a position to crush the competition when you begin the search for a *new first paycheck.*

Another trap is that we fail to recognize the *routine* activities that we do daily, weekly, or monthly as accomplishments. These activities are far from special to anyone else. However, they make you *feel good,* which gives you the confidence to keep pushing forward, knowing that they will produce results.

One of the biggest accomplishments I achieve every week is on Thursday afternoons. It's an activity that *could make money.* I host, along with my awesome co-host, a professional network marketing group and about forty to sixty people attend every week. It's a great experience that allows professionals to meet other people, schedule meetings, and grow businesses. I've been doing this for about ten years and every Thursday night, when I drive home, I take some time to recognize the accomplishment of the day. I helped forty to sixty people *that day* to grow their business! I go to bed that night with the confidence to continue leading that group every week.

This accomplishment allows me to focus on the connections I have made, the trust I have developed, and my previously established relationships. I know that at some point there will be an opportunity to help someone with a real estate project. I know that all of these efforts will bring in revenue at some point, and have accepted that you may wait a long time for that opportunity. I don't just host this group for one week and wonder why I didn't get business. I host it *every* week. I keep showing up! And if you need a pat on the back? Give yourself one! Don't wait for someone to give you one, rather just know, and remember: *do what you love to do, put in the hard work, and the money will come.*

But what if it doesn't? That's a faith thing. You have to stay strong in your hard work and continue to believe that the results you want will happen. In the meantime, there are accomplishments that you achieve all the time that you can hang your hat on, overlooked by many as simple chores.

Maybe you went to the gym four out of seven days. That's an accomplishment! Maybe you mowed the lawn and it looks amazing as you light a campfire at sunset. That's an accomplishment! Maybe you deep cleaned the house and you go to sleep completely relaxed, waking up refreshed the next morning. That, for sure, is an accomplishment!

You get the idea. I had a client who bought a beautiful home in the mountains a few years back, and he unfortunately got laid off from his job. During the time between jobs, he used the scaffolding that came with the house to paint the entire house. By himself. He told me after he got his new job that painting his house during that break was one of the biggest accomplishments he ever achieved because he did the hard work.

REWARDS AND EXPERIENCES

The *experiences*. That's the fun part of accomplishments! You get to do things as a result of all of your hard work. Some of these experiences are in the form of rewards given to you, and some of them are the things you choose to do to enhance your quality of life for you and your family, like taking vacations, going to ball games, concerts, etc. Sometimes the experiences are scheduled, like planning that vacation, but sometimes they are unexpected too.

When I was moving through the ranks at Hooters, as I mentioned, I was fortunate to attend a lot of unforgettable events, including a couple of Super Bowls. The local vendors and distributors had large marketing budgets, and it was just part of their operation to give tickets away, and hope the managers and directors would in return put their "product" on tap. In this case it was beer, and Hooters sold *a ton* of it. This company always ranked in the top 5% in beer sold on these types of restaurant accounts. So, we were in the top 5% of tickets being given, and not just tickets, *good* tickets, like suites, VIP areas, lower levels; you get the idea. I called it "Tickets for Taps," because as the tickets became more in demand as the Hooters concept was growing, managers were changing out brands quicker than Garth Brooks could belt out the third verse of "Friends in Low Places."

My take was just always to sell a lot of beer and grow sales, and if there was a reward for all of the hard work, all the better.

Many people rarely get to experience events like this, where the money is great and the experiences are phenomenal, so I consider myself fortunate as I reflect on the memories. One event in particular stood out as I was growing in the company. I was being promoted and relocating to different markets. I was working hard to drive results, and it's amazing to reflect on all of the rewards that I experienced, including free tickets to concerts, NBA games, NHL games, and NFL games. I even got to go on fishing trips with luxury suite accommodations. Everything was essentially VIP status and every seat at every game was great. One particular event though, was one I had never expected.

It was a summer day in June and my brother was in town. I was living in Michigan, and I had tickets with pit passes to go to the NASCAR race at Michigan International Speedway, which I had never done. At the time, NASCAR was exploding in popularity and these races had crowds of over 150,000 people, with fans tailgating for several days on the infield when their market hosted the race.

My brother and I checked into the pit area to pick up our passes when the beer rep came up to me and said, "Meet me here at 12:15," 45 minutes before the race.

We did and he took us up to the grandstand right behind the start/finish line. He said wait here, and *that* guy down there will motion for you in about 15 minutes, prior to the start of the race. *That* guy was a race official. "OK," I said. "What is that guy going to have me do?"

"You are waving the Green Flag to start the race!"

My brother screamed with excitement, and I was astonished. "Are you serious? How is that going to work?" I asked.

The beer rep responded, "Just do what he tells you and it will be one of the coolest things you have ever done."

Sure enough, with about 10 minutes to go before the race, the official pointed to me and motioned me down. My brother was screaming with excitement as I approached him and looked up at the packed stands full of fans. We stepped out on the small catwalk over the track. I was about to wave the green flag to start the race!

We were up there as the announcer said "Drivers start your engines" and as the cars were doing the warm up, the official told me what was going to happen. "They will come around once and I will put my hand up with one finger when there is one lap before the race starts. I want *you* to stand right here in front, and wave the green flag in a circular motion, *when I tell you*. There are two things. 'Do not wave the flag until I tell you!' and 'Don't drop the flag!'"

Now I was getting nervous. I remember asking, "How will I know when to wave the flag?"

"You will know."

His finger went up as the cars came through, one lap before the green flag.

As the drivers made their way around, the announcer came on saying, "Our green flag is being waved by Brent Rittersdorf." I looked back and my brother was all thumbs up and the crowd was waiting for the start!

The cars came out of Turn 4, and the official had his hand up in a "Not yet" motion. *Not yet, Not yet, not yet*....... NOW! He yelled and punched me in the side! I waved that flag as hard as I could in a furious motion and the cars were screaming by the start line! There was nothing like waving that flag as those thirty or so cars crossed that start line. Once done, I got to stand up there for a couple of laps. The speed of those cars at 180 miles created a bouncing feeling from air movement, and as I shook the hand of the official when done and walked up the stands to my brother, my mind was blown. It was an experience to remember for a lifetime.

Was that really an accomplishment? *Yes.* It was an accomplishment because I put in the hard work, and was recognized by the vendor as such and rewarded. I didn't ask to get picked for this reward. Had I just shown up to the race and my name was picked raffle style, that would have still been an amazing experience for sure. But there is something different about the feeling of getting the reward by doing the work. It feels better and it lasts longer.

Just like my client who did all that scaffolding work to his house to paint it. He *could* have afforded to pay someone to paint it. Easily. But he did all that hard work himself. The feeling would have been great had he paid someone. But the true emotion of doing the work yourself trumps all.

DON'T FORGET THE TRAP!

Just like the first trap above, if you take for granted that these experiences will continue, you may not like the person you become. That person receives free tickets to the game and asks "Where are the seats?" If they're not on the lower level, you turn them down or feel insulted that you were not offered more expensive seats. Ask me how I could possibly know this? Because that was me. I expected that people would give me things and that the experiences continue.

When you put into perspective the accomplishments in *your* journey, think about the times you took for granted those accomplishments. It may humble you a bit. What are some of the unexpected accomplishments in your journey? How did that make you feel? I continuously think about how I can leverage those moments to achieve my expected accomplishments, and not take any of them for granted.

I eventually learned this lesson myself. Going to football and baseball games is important to me, but I learned that the reward of my hard work would allow me to *buy* my own season tickets, and not rely, or expect anyone to give them to me. I bought season tickets to the Atlanta Falcons, and partial season tickets to the Atlanta Braves. They were, and still are not, the best seats. They were not on the club level or in a luxury suite. But they were *mine*. I didn't receive them through my employer. I bought them with my own money, through the true accomplishments I achieved without taking anything for granted. Finally, as a bonus, I get to give many of my seats away to friends and clients. For me, that's an accomplishment.

Accomplishments are the wins in your life as you go 10 for 10. Remember the process as we start. Only *you* can take the shot. This will help you put into perspective the *wins* when you achieve your accomplishments, as well as the *losses* when you fall short, or miss the shot.

I hate losing. But *I love* going 10 for 10.

I'm not going to pour you a shot, but you are about to take several of them!

the shots
GOING 10 FOR 10

shot one
HOPES AND DREAMS

Most people never get to live out their dreams. That sucks. Why is that, and how can that be? Maybe that's because they don't take any action to begin with. The first shot in going 10 for 10 is easy to do, yet difficult if you don't get off your ass and step up to the line.

I had been dreaming that one day I would write this book. That said, I really didn't have a plan to execute it, other than just writing some notes here and there. I was listening to all of the outside noise from everyone that had their take on writing a book. Some said I needed a book. Others said it didn't matter if I had a book or not. Some said I should use a voice recorder and translate it to text. Some even encouraged me to use Chat GPT to write the book. (That seemed and still seems like cheating to me—and my editor is very glad I didn't go this route!) All that said, the dream was going to die if I didn't have some hope (help) to get me started.

I could dream all day about writing a book, but if I don't execute the plan and actually start writing *my* book would never happen. When I decided that I was actually going to complete this project, I knew that for me, there was only going to be one way to write it, and that is the old-fashioned way of sitting in front of a word document and typing the damn thing myself. I could at least get started by writing an outline by consolidating all of those pages of yellow pad notes. From there, I could begin to weave in the stories that would illustrate the points in the Purpose.

But the part that kept me from thinking that this dream would never get to be lived out was that I didn't understand or know the process of actually making a book a reality, that you are holding now. I wanted something more than just a professional business card priced at around $20 that ended up at 200 pages. What do most people do with business cards? By and large, they throw them away!

In order to create a book that had real value and could help, rather than a product that's easily commoditized, I had to actually work at it. If it seems like it's hard, it's supposed to be. Many of the most fulfilling aspects of life come through hard work. And the first step of that process is starting.

Or in the process of 10 for 10, simply stepping up to the line.

HERE'S THE BALL

The first shot may be one of two scenarios. The first is that it's the first time you have ever taken the shot to achieve your greater Purpose. The second is that you are back here because you have missed one of the shots along the way! That's OK. Whether this is your first shot ever, because you're curious to see what could happen with your hopes and dreams, or because of a miss (failure) in your journey, everyone should be able to live out their dreams, and you have to start somewhere.

When you take that first shot, the release of the ball creates an emotion on the line of "Just give me a chance." You want to achieve great things, and like all great hopes and dreams, it's all about getting the chance, or opportunity to just get up there and give it a try. Remember the goal in order to achieve your greater Purpose is to make 10 in a row, and you can't get to 10 without making *one*.

All of those yellow pad pages had stories I wanted to tell! But when it came down to writing this book, I knew I was on the Hopes and Dreams shot because I had never done this before. And the more I looked at all of those pieces of paper, not knowing how to glue them together, they just sat there.

Shot 1 *could* be as simple as buying a lottery ticket. In order to have *hope* you will win the lottery, you have to actually buy a ticket. Before you can *dream* of what you would do with the big jackpot, you have to be able to have that ticket in your pocket.

Even if you miss the shot and your lottery ticket isn't a winner, at least you had the hopes and dreams while you had the ticket, anticipating what could be. If you are like me, you will buy another one because it's worth having those hopes and dreams. All of us need hopes and dreams to hold on to-achievements and experiences to look forward to.

When you discover that your Lottery ticket is a loser, you throw it away. When you win you keep it of course! All of those yellow pieces of paper just sat there on my desk for a long time because I needed to get back to work on other things. Writing the book wasn't important enough to pursue the dream. Yet. And then one day, I looked at the pile of notes and realized they were all winning tickets. It was time to start cashing them in! Time to step up to the line.

TURN UP THE RADIO

When I was fourteen, I was determined to have the *best* stereo on the block. I had gone into the local audio video store and scoped it all out. There was no Best Buy in those days, or Circuit City, which had come and gone. It was just a local store and they showed me the amplifier, the pre-amplifier, the record player, the tape player, and of course the speakers.

In order to buy the stereo, I needed about 1,000 bucks. My parents were not going to give me the money, so I had to get a job. I didn't want to mow lawns or deliver papers like most kids were doing. My brother delivered newspapers every morning, and I don't know how he did it, especially in January. McDonald's was a popular place for everyone's first job, but I had my eyes set on my favorite place. Pizza Hut. I rode my bike down to the superintendent's office and got the paperwork to work as a minor, which of course had all kinds of restrictions of hours, duties, etc.

I went into Pizza Hut, with the *hopes and dreams* of getting a job. I walked in that afternoon and asked to speak to someone in charge. When I was asked *why* by another employee, I indicated that I wanted to apply for a job. They returned my ambition with a look of disgust, as they prompted the manager, who came out and said "Have a seat."

I was ready! My mom had helped me build a resume, which was basically that I was a good student, had done odd jobs like clearing brush, pulling weeds in gardens, moving wood, etc. The manager asked, "Why do you want to work at Pizza Hut?"

"Because Pizza Hut is my favorite, and I want to have the best stereo system on the block. I have a resume and the paperwork from the superintendent's office."

"What do you think you can do here?"

"Make pizza?"

"No," she chuckled. "You aren't old enough. You would be able to wash dishes only by hand, since you are not old enough to use any equipment, and mostly bus tables on weekend nights."

"Does this mean cleaning the tables after people are done eating?"

Another chuckle.

"I clean the table after dinner every night so I can do that."

"How long do you think it takes to bus a table?"

I had to think about that. I never had a job like this before so I really had no idea. And I had never really thought about that part of the service. Clearly, on my trips to Pizza Hut, I was mostly concerned with eating pizza and never paid attention.

"It can't take more than *ten* minutes."

This time she burst out laughing.

"OK." She said, "Come back on Friday and we will give you a chance."

Hopes and Dreams achieved! I did have the chance to work at Pizza Hut and was on my way to the stereo. I did find that it really didn't take 10 minutes to bus a table, and learned how to cook pizzas too. (Don't tell the superintendent!)

Another Hope and Dream I had was to learn how to play the guitar. I actually was given a beautiful acoustic guitar for my thirtieth birthday. I bought the books to learn, as well as the stand. I could envision myself playing a Springsteen song!

And to this day it sits on the stand. I have tried many times to figure it out and I just can't get my fingers to do what the chord says, or my brain to understand how to read the notes of what to do. I guess you could say learning how to play the instrument still remains in the "Land of Hopes and Dreams."

If you never take the Hopes and Dreams shot, you'll never know whether your goal is worth pursuing. If you miss the shot, you're OK with it because you won't have regrets if you don't pursue it. I would have loved to learn how to play guitar, but my life is still going to be full and complete even without this skill. In order to learn this, though, we have to step up to the line and take the shot. Not every attempt goes in, but we learn about what truly motivates us through this first step. If you don't attempt the first shot, you will never know.

Even without the skills to play the guitar myself, I still have the turntable from that original stereo, which has since been refurbished, along with several old records, one of which is indeed "Born in the USA" by the Boss himself!

STARTING THE PROCESS

Regardless of how successful you will be in going 10 for 10, *everyone* starts at Shot 1. Every successful job often starts with an interview, whether you're thirteen applying to make pies at Pizza Hut or fifty-three and looking to break into the C-suite. Every time you start the process, there may be some anxiety because this process is hard, and as you get older, there's more stuff to lose.

The emotions, and even anxiety, may start out more nonchalant if you don't get a positive response from that first job interview, but can become significant as you move up the ladder.

All of us are on the line at some point. Because everyone deserves to have Hopes and Dreams.

shot two
GOOD LUCK

The excitement and curiosity of making the Hopes and Dreams shot has propelled you to the line to take Shot 2, The Good Luck shot. There is a slight shift, though. You are at the line about to attempt the shot and you realize that *you are being watched.*

That's the emotion on the line. The awareness of being observed. While it is true that everyone is saying "Good Luck," the inference is drastically different. Half of the people want you to succeed. The other half probably are not taking you seriously yet and would not be surprised if you fail. Some may even *hope you fail.*

The words "good luck" may not specifically be used, but you will immediately know the reference. Picture your favorite aunt or grandmother who is older and you tell her something positive. Her response?

"Bless your Heart!"

Now tell her something negative. Her response?

"Bless Your Heart"

Same words. Two completely different meanings!

The shot begins to create your *credibility* which is not yet established. The key here on the Good Luck shot is that you are still new to the game. Your 10 for 10 experience is just beginning. Keep the people who are your cheerleaders close to you! Those who don't take you seriously *eventually* will. That may be the most challenging part of this shot, to block out the noise of those who don't take you seriously. That doesn't mean you are not respectful to them or listen for cues that you can learn from. You do, however, shut off the speaker inside your head that keeps telling you all the reasons why you can't go 10 for 10. Sure, success can be hard to achieve and sustain. Failure is easy, because you can give up any time.

The Good Luck shot shows no mercy, mostly because we only hear the doubters around us that assume, or even cheer, for failure. It may not be intentional, like at a sports event where you want the other team to fail, but it's there nonetheless.

THE NEW GUY

My restaurant career was very eventful, and I got the opportunity to travel a lot, and move to many different cities. Atlanta, Orlando, Miami, Jacksonville and Detroit to name a few. To that end, when I lived in Atlanta and traveled to cities in the Midwest, Northeast, and Southeast, I had the opportunity to see a lot of different markets.

With that came many promotions, or changes, in territory. Some of these changes involved a change in title, some involved a change in territory. But they all involved a change in people in some way. I realized that every time one of these changes happened, I was *the new guy.*

In every *new* job that I have had, there were certainly people that were happy for me. The hiring manager, my new boss, the executive team, and support teams were all excited for me to get plugged in. There was always that first day when those supporting people were saying "Good luck!" because they wanted me to be a great addition to the company.

In every *existing* job that I have had, the executive team promoting me or transferring me all felt the same way. They knew I had the talent to get results in a new role or territory, and hence they too, were all saying "Good luck!" as I loaded all my shit in the moving truck or booked the plane ticket to a new market.

Do you know how many times the red carpet was rolled out for my first day at the restaurant? None. I was always *the new guy.* And while all of those who had supported me wished me "good luck" in the new role, *they* were not the people I would manage or work with. I was accountable for the employees. They were all saying "good luck," too, but it always had a different tone. Existing employees would look at me skeptically: *He's the new guy but we've seen this before. We have been here long before him and we will be here long after he's gone.*

Some of the peers were happy for me of course but still others were not. Some were jealous that they didn't get the promotion. Some were nervous because of possible changes I would make, because not only was I the new guy, their *old guy* was gone. I hadn't even started day one yet! No matter whether a brand new job or a change within, I was *always* the new guy at some point.

It was on me to prove to them through my leadership that I was here to help, and over time win them over and calm their concerns. In 10 for 10, there are always going to be people that are rooting for you and your success, yet there will be others who are skeptical and could not care less. They would not be surprised if you fail. Most of the time this is because they just don't know you, so it's easy to form an opinion based on little knowledge—or none at all. Their perception of you is based on the opinions of others, until you personally invest in the time to know them.

In my case, I took the time to get to know the people I was working with, over a coffee, beer, or staying after meetings to chat. It's amazing how much you learn about people and their values over simple one-on-one conversations. In an increasingly online world, it's so easy to form opinions about people whom we don't even know. The best way to show people your true self is to, well, show them. There's an adage about leadership that "People don't care how much you know, until they know how much you care." That line has been prescient for my entire time leading teams, especially in the often stressful restaurant industry.

Your job is to get as many people to invest in that success because when you win, or make the shot, everyone else wins too.

SHE'S BEEN A REALTOR FOR 30 YEARS

I had only started my full time career in real estate when I was asked to go to a business association expo. This was an expo that featured many local business-es of all kinds of trades and services, like financial planning, plumbing, electrical, mortgage lenders, etc., and of course, real estate. My colleague and I set up our table and not long after the event started, this tall guy, probably in his sixties, walked up to me and said, "So, you do real estate, do you?"

"Yes. Nice to meet you. I'm Brent and I'm looking forward to meeting many people today."

"How long have you been doing real estate?"

"Well, I have been licensed for a few years, and just started this full time, as I realize that this is not a part-time job for me."

He just looked at me and handed me a business card with the picture of a woman on it. "Well, my wife has been a realtor for thirty years and is one of the top producers in the area. She is the best around. This is not an easy job to have and most people I meet are out of the business within a year. It was nice to meet you. Good LUCK."

I walked back to our expo table thinking "What kind of bullshit was that?" I was pissed and ready for the event to be over and go home. He had succeeded in screwing with my mind, and I'm sure that doubt came through as I worked my networking table for the rest of the night. But I was *young* in my 10 for 10 experience. I didn't have confidence in myself yet, so I let it affect me. My credibility was not established. But as I experienced 10 for 10, that credibility did grow, as well as my personal resolve to give a different response to that "good luck" guy.

As I drove home that night, I kept replaying his words and I admit, wondered if I was going to be one of the people he knew that was out of the business in a year. He would be right, and I would be starting over. This would have been a perfect time to cue up Springsteen's "Land of Hopes and Dreams." I needed the motivation in order to get me past this doubt and embrace the sacrifices I would need to make to keep going and prove him wrong.

When I did get home, I found the business card of the woman that the guy had given me. "She's been a realtor for 30 years". I looked at the picture. It was a beautiful young woman. I looked at the picture again. There was *no way* the person in this picture had been doing real estate for thirty years! I burst out laughing.

To this day, anytime I hear the words "I've been a realtor for..... years," I am reminded of that event, and just laugh to myself. The humor allows me to focus on my "cheerleaders" of support and block out words of inflection that cast doubt.

SOME SACRIFICE WILL BE REQUIRED

The lesson on shot 2 is Promise. The sacrifice, remember? The miss gives you the experience of starting over, which is the consequence of a missed shot. When you miss the shot, you have to start back at the beginning. The *new guy* on his first day may have had a real shitty start when no red carpet was rolled out. The *new guy* woke up the next day and went back to work and actually got to start his first day *again* as the noise from the previous day subsided and the attention was "back to work" for everyone else. The *new guy* had to make a sacrifice of time to get to know his people.

I had to sacrifice my *pride* with the guy who told me *"good luck"* in real estate, and keep the promise to myself that I would keep focused on what I knew how to do and not focus on the doubt of others.

Remember, Promise means that you acknowledge you will have to sacrifice something in order to achieve it. It became clear to me when I experienced it, too. Focus on the positive energy from your supporters and push aside the negative emotions from others. That means avoid the gossip, assumptions, jokes, and all that other shit that is just noise.

For a while, you may feel strange, even lonely as you work through this promise. You are not alone, because everyone, even the doubters, have been there before. This is your greater Purpose. How you choose to live 10 for 10, is up to *you*.

shot three
WHAT THE HELL?

That *loneliness feeling* drives you to give up. Whether it's in a meeting absorbing the content, or being the presenter delivering the keynote, it can be isolating. Communicating with others and not feeling like you are in the right group can make you feel lonely. Spending a ton of time on a project that doesn't get results, can definitely make you feel lonely. In fact, any experience in your life that gives you a gut feeling of loneliness, and leaves you wondering whether a change may have to take place, is a good indication that you are on Shot 3: What the hell.

All of this can lead to doubt and exhaustion. When you are exhausted, you just want to give up. To be clear, being *exhausted* is different from being *tired.* When you are tired, you have put in a great day of work life balance, and while your gas tank is empty, you know how and where to fill up the tank to recharge. However when you are exhausted, you have put in a ton of work, but you question the results (if any) and fail to *recharge* the tank, leaving you still tired the next day. Back to the line, if you will. You have been going through the motions now so many times and attempted this "shot," and it just doesn't go in. You are at the point of saying "I give up." Congratulations. What the hell.

MAINE TO MIAMI

One of my first experiences of the What the Hell shot came after I was out of college. I hated college, and probably never should have gone. To this day, there is not one person I remember from college, can call and have a beer with, or even share a social media post with. I only went for two years and got an associate degree in Hotel Restaurant Management. In high school, I knew I wasn't excited to attend college, but went to satisfy the norm by going down the path of working hard, making money and being happy. This started with The University of Southern Maine.

In fact, the father of the girl whom I was dating at the time was the one who kept me in college. He *rarely* spoke to me the whole time his daughter and I were dating, even though I was over at her house all the time. I don't think it was because he didn't like me, I think it was just because he rarely spoke at all. But this one fall afternoon on a school break, we were in the kitchen of her house and he was there and did speak to me. He asked me how college was, and I said I hated it. In fact, I said I wanted to give up. He then proceeded to ask what I would do if I quit college, and I said something like I would just bartend full-time as that's what I loved doing, and made a lot of friends there.

He stopped what he was doing and walked over to me. He was tall and it was the closest in distance that I had ever been to him.

He said, "Go back, and stay in college."

"Why?"

"Life is like a shit sandwich. The bigger the bite, the worse it will taste. Go the *fuck back to college*."

And he walked out of the room. There were probably a half dozen or more people in the kitchen that day as the rest of the family had friends over from school break too. But the room was silent for several moments. *What the hell.* I went back to college.

I *did* graduate and went back to my small hometown in Maine. It was great, as I was bartending at night and playing basketball during the day. I *still* felt the same way about college, but it was about finishing what I started—and it seemed like a better alternative than eating a *shit sandwich*. Back in my hometown in Maine, as I was bartending and playing basketball, I had a ton of friends from work whom I would hang out with during the day on the court before work at night.

Cappy's Chowder House was on 1 Main St. in Camden, Maine. It literally was like going to Cheers, where everyone knew your name and if you got to work there, you were in good company. The friends I never made in college? They came from Cappy's. I learned how to wait tables, bartend, and even some administrative skills, all well making some of the best friends and experiences to go with it. I still connect with some of them today. I think the bind was that while Cappy's thrived in the summer with all of the tourists and part-time staff, (and a crazy owner with a temper that would cause her to throw things in anger when things went wrong like keys, coffee cups, even a vacuum cleaner!), we survived in the off season when business was slower and it was just a core staff that supported each other.

There was no *degree* from working there, but if you have ever worked in a restaurant, you have earned one nonetheless.

But something happened about a year after that in this small town. I was playing basketball and began to notice that the same guys were playing every day. After a while, I noticed there were new guys in the group too. It was for a variety of reasons. Some graduated high school and didn't go to college. They were going to work locally. Some came back from college (with fancier degrees than me), and went to work locally. There were also some guys that had been playing there for years. It occurred to me that *they were never going to leave.*

While gaining seniority at the restaurant, now working the best shifts and even doing some minor managerial functions, I learned through conversations about how some of the staff were living. They were always looking to pick up shifts to make rent. They were speaking of how they were going to have to potentially get another job to pay for the health insurance. They became threatened when someone new got hired, gossiping that they may lose a shift here or there. *They were never going to leave.*

I began to wonder if that would be me, too. Was that all I was supposed to do? If so, would I be content with that? The girlfriend from that day in the kitchen was long gone, but the words from her dad and the shit sandwich resurfaced. Was this the plan? Ultimately the answer was no, and then the next question arose. "What the hell am I doing here?" *I had to leave.*

And that's what I did. I packed up all of my stuff that I could put into my truck, and started driving. Away from Maine. And when I was finished, I was in Miami. I enrolled in an audio visual production technical school, worked at the Marriott, and even refereed some high school basketball games. Talk about games being played above the rim! I was working freshman games with kids who could dunk.

And me? Here I was, in South Beach. The bars in Maine closed at 1 a.m. at the latest, yet on South Beach, you could hear music from the bars until 4 a.m. I was driving a Jeep truck with a Maine license plate with roll bar lights, spotlights, and a custom-made truck bed cover out of wood that my dad made, that when locked, no one would be able to break into. There was *nothing* even close to resemble it. I was not able to speak a lick of Spanish. A fish out of water? Hell yes!

Now, I was at a crossroads going 10 for 10. I had been on the what the hell shot still living in Maine, and fearful that I may miss out on growth opportunities causing this massive move. There couldn't have been more drastic of a change. The only thing that was the same was the Interstate 95 sign that literally runs the length of the east coast. Even the salt water of the Atlantic Ocean, while still the same body of water, was different. The temperature of the warmer water and sound of long cresting waves sent me crashing back to Shot 1, Hopes and Dreams, to start something new.

Here comes the jacked-up part though. I missed home! I didn't have any friends! I would grab an empanada and a tall cold beer from the convenience store and walk to the beach and just look north to where I had come from. How could it be possible I would miss the colder water temperatures as the waves exploded on the granite beaches? Excited as I was to try new things, I thought about the basketball games at the rec center I was missing. The bartender shifts I was missing. The alternative was to stay in Maine of course and potentially keep missing Shot 3, or give this new chapter in life a "go" and reach new milestones. I wasn't sure. But as I finished that forty-ounce beer as the sun was setting, many nights I would say *"What the Hell am I doing!"*

I have met so many people who made new moves to a new area, and I know that at some point the question of "what the hell" has been asked. You can tell by listening to them and watching their body language as they talk about where they came from and the successes that they had there. The moves aren't as drastic as Maine to Miami; some of them are just one or two towns or counties away. But the doubt of whether you will be successful in this new area is real. The exhaustion is real too. I think we *all* have *moved* from "Maine to Miami" at some point.

Sometimes though, those long drive decisions are not made up of your own volition. Sometimes they are made *for* you.

JACKSONVILLE TO DETROIT

Jacksonville, Florida, in the winter is nice. Maybe not as nice as Miami. But, certainly nicer than, say, Detroit. Yet, that is where I found myself and my dad that January week, driving a U-Haul with a car carrier and a jet ski of all things, from Florida to Michigan. I had been "promoted" by Hooters to move from Jacksonville to Detroit at the company's end of year conference just a few weeks earlier in December.

Unlike some promotions, I had no idea this was on the near horizon. I had only been in the position in Jacksonville for about eight months, and was really starting to enjoy it. It was a new role for me, and as an area supervisor over five restaurants, I was learning management skills on a whole new level. Some of the perks were good too. I had been given four suite tickets to the Florida-Georgia football game, which was dubbed at the time the "World's Largest Outdoor Cocktail Party." The contest is a fall staple in Jacksonville, played around Halloween every fall and one of the most anticipated games on the college schedule annually.

In December, I drove to Atlanta from Jax. The drive was only six hours, and on this ride, the temperature went from sixty degrees to thirty-four as I drove up for a convention. I had barely checked into the hotel when my boss asked me to meet him in the lobby. That's when they "promoted" me, and while I had a choice, I really didn't. Merry Christmas! An Area Supervisor over five restaurants in Jacksonville would now serve as an Area Supervisor over five to seven restaurants in Detroit. If you are thinking that seems more like a lateral move, you are not alone. But it was sold as a promotion and another step to being promoted to a Divisional Vice President, and if you could manage an out of market region with little supervision... you get the idea. So I packed up all of my shit again, including the jet ski, and then made the eighteen-hour drive from Jacksonville to Detroit.

The night before we left, we were in a hot tub in 60-degree weather. The day we left, we got caught in a winter storm that brought driving rain through Valdosta, and snow with white out conditions in Ohio. And as we entered Detroit, with snow falling, I cast my eyes on a giant industrial smokestack spewing out fire with green and black smoke. We moved into my new apartment on a twenty-degree day with the snow still falling, and my dad and I laughed as we slid that damn jet ski down the aluminum ramp from the moving truck. That jet ski was the *last* thing I would be using for a while. The first thing I needed, however, was a shovel.

What the Hell am I doing!

For sure, I was wondering if this "promotion" was more like a "demotion". The person who took over my region appeared to have gotten the better end of the deal.

While self doubt, or perhaps selfishness, indeed creeps in on this part of your 10 for 10 experience, being in touch with what it looks and feels like helps you identify the situation. When you acknowledge your own "what the hell" moments, the lesson becomes easier to embrace and act on. You may even laugh along the way.

KEEP *MOVING FORWARD*

How can you get past this shot when things seem so dark? How can there possibly be light at the end of this tunnel?

PROMISE. Remember the promise you made to yourself to achieve your greater Purpose. Remember to acknowledge that there will be sacrifices you make in order to achieve your Purpose and get beyond Shot 3. These sacrifices will evolve and even grow from Shot 2 (Good Luck), but they are still sacrifices. The challenge in the Good Luck shot was distancing yourself from the doubt of others.

In Shot 3, you must distance yourself from self-doubt. Only you can make the promise to you that *you* matter, you will put in the hard work, and embrace the sacrifices. It doesn't matter whether you *choose* to move from "Maine to Miami," or if you are *told* to move from "Jacksonville to Detroit."

The sacrifices of attempting new challenges will make you feel uncomfortable. They are, however, part of your experience and ultimately will get you closer to your Purpose.

How can the What the Hell shot help *you*?

Accept that you can't escape it. Embrace the suck. Enjoy the pain. Laugh—especially at the jet ski you brought to Michigan which you will no longer need.

At the same time, you will create memories of a lifetime. I will never forget those days drinking a beer on South Beach looking at the ocean. I will always remember that sun-to-snow move with my Dad. The memories and emotions of the sacrifices you make may initially be painful. And while initially creating the feeling to give up, the ultimate direction is to *move forward*.

shot four
ROUTINE

When I wake up in the morning, I make the bed first thing before anything else. Then I check the phone to make sure there were no emergencies overnight, take my vitamins, spend some time in prayer, then a cup of coffee over sports highlights, the to-do list for the day, emails, and then go to the gym or to work depending on the day.

Welcome to my boring life, which probably mirrors yours as well.

The Routine shot, which is the fourth shot on your 10 for 10 experience, actually does sound "boring." It seems pretty self-explanatory on its surface. Routine. Do what you are supposed to do when you are supposed to do it and you will be successful. Morning routine. Work routine. Family routine. Chores-around-the-house routine.

When you take the Routine shot, the emotion on the line as you release the ball is *focus.* You are dialed in on all of the details. You are serious about being perfect, and your mindset is that "I get to do this" rather than "I have to do this." The details are critical and you want to know all of them. When you go 10 for 10, the Routine shot is the most valuable shot on the board in order to be perfect and achieve your greater Purpose.

This is where you need a coach of some sort. The coach, mentor, advisor, boss, book, tutorial, etc. is critical in helping you with the Routine shot. Why? Because they have been there. They have done it, experienced it, or written about it. They know the details , and in some cases, your coach probably has forgotten more about the subject than you could ever learn.

ARE YOU READY?

When I was organizing the shots for the 10 for 10 experience, and naming them, I had all these 3x5 index cards, with the shots listed on each one. I would put them on the table and move them around to organize them. For a long time, Routine was the first shot. That made sense at first because everyone needs a routine, and most successful people I know have one. To that point, the most successful people I know *embrace* the routine and look forward to the boring parts of their day so that they can accomplish their objectives. Every night I would get home and look at those index cards, with Routine as Shot 1, and something felt wrong.

One night when I came home from work late, I looked at the index cards and moved it to the fourth slot. It was perfect and the question was quickly answered: *you* are not ready for the Routine shot until shot 4.

Assume for a moment, though, it was Shot 1. If I gave you all the details and specifics of a job, task, system, etc., right away, that doesn't mean you will be good at it, because you were not ready to learn about it yet. This may *not* be something you want to do, (Hopes and Dreams), and you have not *promised* yourself that you want to take the time (Sacrifice) to learn the details. You have to want it first, which will make your routine more powerful. Hence, the order makes more sense by introducing routine further down the line.

Remember the original 10 for 10 back in High School? My coach didn't teach me the details on how to make free throws on the first day of tryouts. He made me (and everyone) run. We ran sprints. We ran suicides. We ran drills, many times without a ball. Then we would run again. Coach wasn't going to teach us the details, until it was clear that we were even going to make the team. And I almost *didn't* make the team. I had to tell the coach I wanted to be on varsity, knowing I might rarely play. Sure, I attempted free throws in practice, but I wasn't ready to learn the details. I was still on those early shots keeping the promise to myself that I would keep running those drills, and not playing while all the other kids on the junior varsity team got to play. I wasn't ready for the details yet, and Coach wasn't going to teach me the details until he knew I was ready.

But he did teach them- one day after practice- with a lot of running.

AHA ON THE LINE

I know I said this isn't a book solely about basketball, but in order to illustrate the importance of routine, the details and the coaching involved, I have to step on the court for a moment to make the point. Forgive me!

Coach came up to me one day when I was on the foul line. I was going to take a free throw and he stopped me. He taught me that there was a nail in the center of the foul line on the court. He taught me to put my left foot just to the right of the center of that nail. Since I am left-handed, this was the best way to line up the shot. He taught me how to hold the ball and to shoot the ball only with one hand, as the right hand is just a guide on the side. It should not be involved in the shooting motion as it will change the course of the shot and create a miss. He taught me how to create a pattern of how many times to bounce the ball to prepare for the shot. In my case, it was five. He encouraged me to look at the basket after those bounces and to look at the same spot on the rim. He taught me to breathe and then how to release the ball, holding my shooting arm steady as the shot left, and watch the ball go in. And if it didn't,

I had to ask myself "What did the ball do?" and reverse my motions to find where I made the mistake. *Routine!* This included all of the actions leading up to taking the shot, the actual motions of taking the shot, and understanding the reactions of how the ball went into the basket. Or, in the case of a miss, how the ball would bounce off for the rebound. (Coach would later teach me how to position myself for a rebound and my important role in securing boards as a supporting player.)

This is why the Routine shot is so valuable. Whatever job you are in, you must learn the details if you want to be successful. But you can't learn the details until you *want* to learn them. You have to love the job, and know what sacrifices of time initially you will have to make to learn those details. And over time those details become *habits* which fuel the routine. You can read a shit ton of books about habits, but for me, and you, when you are *ready* to learn the details, your Routine will be the most powerful tool you have in going 10 for 10.

That's why a lot of people fail, or struggle with their jobs, or leaders fail at developing teams. The details of the job are focused on *before* the commitment is solid. Just because you got the job, doesn't mean you are any good at it. It just means someone gave you the chance, just like Coach did for me to play (practice) on the varsity team.

This includes all of the actions leading up to taking the shot, and understanding the reactions of what happens when the ball goes in, or out. The rebound.

1099 TO W-2

Do you remember a time in your life when you got your first "real" job? For many, including me, I got my first real job after I had made that crazy trip to Miami. I had left the bartending job in Maine, and while waiting tables for a bit, my first real job was at a Marriott hotel in Miami. It was a true salaried position with a title! I was on my way to the top of Corporate America! And the best part is that I had to wake up at 5 a.m. every day to start work by 6, wear a heavy red polyester jacket (in Miami) and work extra long hours setting up banquet rooms. I was a Catering Service Manager, in charge of the room set up for every meeting function. It was an entry level job at best, and I was making less money (in Miami) than I was in Maine.

This was my opportunity though to get into management. I needed someone to give me the opportunity, and for many of us, those first jobs were just that. An opportunity to get in the organization and learn along the way.

This was my first real test at creating a routine, because no longer was I just pouring drinks, washing glasses, and going home. I had a small staff whom I was in charge of, and got my first exposure to management responsibilities as it related to productivity.

In hotel banquet space, you have meeting rooms, ballrooms, patio space, pool deck space, etc. and the spaces can be configured into larger or smaller spaces based on the size of the crowd. There are also several different kinds of events, from sales presentations, to breakout meetings, to awards dinners, to weddings and receptions. Each one of these has a different setup, with tables, chairs, stages, microphones, dance floors. You get the idea.

What I learned, though, is to have a *routine* to analyze the current setups from previous events, observe the Banquet Event Orders of upcoming occasions, and consolidate existing setups into future ones. The sales managers didn't care that a wedding for a 100 with a dance floor was in Salon AB, but if there was an existing set up for 75 in Salon CD, why move the entire room? Use the existing space and configure it from there, saving time and money.

The biggest shift in routine though was that I no longer had any money! Gone were the days of making cash tips bartending. Here was the more traditional way of getting paid; every two weeks. I had to learn a *new routine* of how to earn, and spend money.

POTATO CAKES

One of the best routines I learned on earning money years later (after the Hooters career) was when I was a Director of Operations job I had at a fast food chain, Arby's. While in training, I had to work the drive through window, taking orders, handling money and talking to people on a headset and through a window. It actually was a very odd experience, because it was so impersonal. Long gone were the days I used to work behind a bar connecting people who were having a good time and spending disposable income. This was different. There was no connecting with people per se, it was just fulfilling a need in the customer's life, as getting fast food was part of *their* routine, whether it be going to or from work, sports practice, meetings, or trying to get a meal on a budget.

I'm at this drive through, and it's in the Northeast, and it's January. That means its f*cking cold with all the fun wind, rain and snow. Do you know what a pain in the ass it's like to handle money and bags of food through a window when it's like that? Your hands are basically numb all day and freezing from the cold. And you are in training, which means you really don't know what you are doing and all of the young sixteen- to twenty-year-olds are running circles around you and most likely are making fun of you.

There was a specific script to be used when taking the order, and part of it was that when any sandwich was ordered, you were supposed to say, "Will that be with large potato cakes?" I thought that was dumb and after saying it about ten times I decided to have more fun with that. "How about a few orders of fries? "Any specific sides?" "Going to get any desserts today? Jamocha shake?" I was all over the board. I thought it was cool.

My VP on a training visit did not. "Why are you not following the script?" he asked. I said it was kind of boring and not fun, reflecting how this was nowhere close to being fun like working in the causal chain environment.

He said- "This is not supposed to be fun. We are here to serve people who are living their lives, and we are part of their routine. If we don't live up to the expectations of their routine, then they will go somewhere else."

"OK, but what about the Potato Cakes part of the script? Why do we have to say that?"

"Because potato cakes have the highest Gross Profit than any other item on the whole menu, and when you sell those consistently, your profitability in the store will excel beyond budget, and your region will rank in the higher tiers of the brand. *Learn the script.*"

Well shit. Details. It was then I began to have respect for that style of the restaurant industry. More important, the details were so important right down to a script around potato cakes. The details made the routine. Let's sell some damn potato cakes! (Arby's brought them back to their menu full time in 2024)

W-2 TO 1099

"You are leaving your job with a guaranteed paycheck to sell real estate?"

"Yes."

"Are you sure that's a good idea?"

"I hope so."

"Good Luck."

So here I was, years later after all of the corporate jobs and experiences, going *back* to where I started. Going from a W-2 job, back to 1099, but this time not a bartender. This time, a Real Estate Broker. I had taken all the tests, gotten the broker license and had all of the support around me to help with the transactions that were yet to come. I had a pretty good awareness of the technology as I had taken some classes and my previous corporate experience had exposed me to several different platforms that I was already familiar with. But there was one thing missing of course. Clients. And I honestly didn't know where they were going to come from.

I knew I needed a routine. I set the calendar up with networking events. Coffee conversations. Training classes. All of it kept me busy. There was one small detail though that I had overlooked.

The Script.

Remember how important the script was for potato cakes? If Arby's could have a detail that was so scripted out to grow business, I needed one to grow *mine.* And years later, my script is: "To help you and your friends make wise decisions in real estate that produce favorable results."

That's the first thing I say at any networking event, or anytime I respond to someone whom I have just met and they ask me what I do. It's the same every time, to the point that people I network a lot with can say it for me.

Routine deserves your attention to all the details, right down to *your* script.

NAILING THE DETAILS

When you embrace all of the details in your routine, you will make this shot and approach the halfway mark of your 10 for 10 experience. The lesson taught here is to have a positive attitude about *Practice*.

Here's how the Routine shot can help you:

Practice all of those details. Every day. Every shift you work. Every call you make. Every email you write. Watch how you execute the details, and then pay attention to how they are received. If they are received positively, keep practicing the same way. If you are not achieving the results you want, fine-tune the details. Just like I knew how to identify the center of the foul line. Just like l learned to observe banquet event space. Just like when I learned that potato cakes were the highest gross profit item on the menu. In business, it's one thing to run the business. But when you master the details, you *know* the business you run.

Every time I go to Arby's and see the sign advertising potato cakes, I smile. Something so minor that helped me perfect routine on a much deeper level is almost downright silly! That said, I guess that looking for a nail in the foul line to position my feet sounds odd, too. If you are learning a routine, or in a leadership position where you are teaching a routine, there is a powerful evolution of *nailing* the details, no matter how silly they seem.

That's the secret to the Routine shot. You will have such an incredible appreciation of all of the details of what your Purpose is that you won't mind taking the time to practice them, tweak them, and pay attention to the results of them. You aren't practicing for the game. You are *practicing* for the practice!

shot five
CONFIDENCE

The sound of silence is eerily amazing and emotional. When you take Shot 5, you feel unstoppable, because you *know* you can make the shot now. Gone are the days of frustration, worrying about what others say, and self-doubt (at least for now). You are keeping your promises, and have developed a killer routine to achieve your greater Purpose.

Up to this point in the 10 for 10 journey, there hasn't been a lot to be excited about. You haven't had a lot of success to this point and, deservedly so, you are ready for it. The hard work is about to pay off as you are close to being *halfway* in going 10 for 10!

There is another emotion too. Pride. Without a doubt, the earlier experiences that challenge you and the promises you had to make fueled that self doubt and humility. Now, though, there is a level of satisfaction because of your performance. It comes because of all the practice you have been doing, and refusal to give up.

One more emotion-eagerness. You look forward to taking this shot because you can't wait to experience the accomplishment. There is a caveat though. Beware of this shot when you make it, because the experience may be different than you anticipate. Why?

The sound of silence is eerily amazing and emotional.

LABOR DAY

I remember when I did my first real estate transaction. I had been doing all the right things, including going to networking events, taking classes, studying the market, making calls, sending out postcards, etc. The only thing I didn't do was put an ad on a bus bench, like Phil Dunphy from *Modern Family!*

I had been doing this all summer and frankly was not getting any positive results. It was frustrating for sure. One of the tactics you are supposed to do is be on social media to let everyone know you sell real estate. And that was "liking" everyone's summer vacations, trips to the beach, Europe, cruises, etc. I really wasn't liking that, especially since the next place I would look was the bank account, as the numbers going out became larger and the numbers coming in were, well, nothing.

The end of the summer was approaching, and it was Friday before Labor Day. Of course, all of the conversations were centered on plans for the long weekend. When they asked me what I was going to do, I said I was going to mow the lawn and do some yard work. I could afford to do that.

Later that day as everyone had left the office, the phone rang. All I remember was the words "We want to sell our house."

Holy shit! I inquired how they got my name and they said it was from a postcard I sent.

Holy shit! They then said "Would you like to see the house so we can discuss? We know it's a holiday weekend and are OK with some time next week."

"I will be there Monday."

"Labor Day?"

"Yes, I look forward to meeting you."

I got the listing! It took about forty-five days to have it listed and under contract, and the closing was approaching. It was the second week of October, and in Atlanta it still can be hot in the afternoon, and that was no exception on this eighty-eight degree day. I had on my brand-new suit jacket and dress shoes. I'm driving to do a quick walkthrough, cold bottle of champagne in the truck, blasting "Unstoppable" by Sia! Let's go to closing!

One problem. My clients were not ready. They had insisted on moving everything themselves, and here we are, an hour before closing and the house is not empty and cleaned yet. Closing is in less than two hours, and the buyer still has yet to do a walk-through. My clients were exhausted and were at the end of their rope.

I took off my jacket, rolled up the sleeves of my brand-new white button down, and started loading. I'm sweating and just doing my best to get the rest of their shit in the truck, empty the house, and run the vacuum. We got it done, drove to the closing, sweaty white dress shirt and all, just in time as the buyers pulled up to do their final walkthrough. We finished closing and as I handed them their bottle of champagne as they got in the moving truck to drive six hours to their new home I said to them "Thank you." They responded, "No, thank *you*."

I got home that night- First commission check in my hand. It felt unreal! I knew that I had accomplished something. I sat in my house and just stared at that check. It was quiet, and I became emotional. I cried. And I just kept staring at it.

The sound of silence is eerily amazing and emotional.

THE OFFICE ON A HOLIDAY

For some reason, I have always gotten *more* done on Labor Day than average. I know that it's a long holiday where people take small vacations, and time off, but for me, I remember more days mowing the lawn, stacking a woodpile, or going to the office for a few hours to knock out a ton of administrative work to get organized ahead of schedule for the days, if not weeks, to come.

I think that's because growing up in Maine, Labor Day, while a day and long weekend off, meant that big changes were on the way. The school year always started the day after Labor Day. While students and teachers have been in school for a month already in the Southern parts of the country, in Maine and other Northern states it always was the day after Labor Day. In turn, the weather also changes. In mid-coast Maine, it changes almost instantly around Labor Day. The nights become notably chillier, and you know that fall is imminent when you see the first leaves on the maple tree change in color.

The leaves aren't the only thing that start to fall off around Labor Day - so does the foot traffic around town. Maine is a summer destination for many people from Boston and New York, and on Labor day, they all *leave* too, because their summer is over and school starts as well. The news channels always would report major backups on the highways as this mass exodus of people were heading south out of the state.

So for me and many, Labor Day was a day of preparation. It was stacking a pile of wood, or getting some extra yard work done before the busy schedules of school commanded our time. Maybe it was getting in a run for the upcoming cross country season, or *even* shooting a few baskets. It was also a nice day for a last bike ride around town, and always one thing stood out as I would ride through Main Street, where just a few days earlier it was packed with people but now they were gone.

The sound of silence is eerily amazing and emotional.

I guess that's why I've always embraced work of some sort on Labor day. While many are on vacation or finishing up one, the time is there for me to get some uninterrupted work done, which prepares me for upcoming events, boosting my confidence of being ready. A couple of hours in the office on Labor Day could equal the equivalent of several days' work during the normal work schedule. Subliminally, that's probably why I was more than happy to visit that client on Labor Day.

WHERE ARE ALL THE CHEERLEADERS?

How can the Confidence shot help you?

The lesson of the confidence shot is accomplishment. It's not a "game winning" shot though, because you are only half way through the 10 for 10 journey. It's kind of a silent win, and while strange at first, it's actually pretty cool to know when it's happening.

The sound of silence is eerily amazing and emotional.

When I got that first commission check, you know how many people called to congratulate me? None.

When I spent those extra hours in the office on Labor Day, you know how many people recognized that? None.

When I stacked that pile of wood on Labor Day, or mowed the yard do you know how many people cared? Why would they?

But the accomplishments were there all the same. No matter how big or small, they gave me confidence. I knew after that first commission check that there would be more based on my hard work. I knew that I was organized to handle the upcoming work load from the extra time in the office. And I knew that that freshly mowed yard with a nice pile of wood stacked, ready for a fire at some point was indeed a level of preparation.

Getting through Shot 5 means you have built a phenomenal foundation to go 10 for 10! The halfway mark is indeed an accomplishment. Embrace the silence, and be attentive of this foundation.

The second half of 10 for 10 is about to start out scary.

shot six
THE SCARY AIRBALL

The only bad thing about control is losing it, and when you take Shot 6, you want your control back. The Scary Airball shot is that part of your life where the emotion on the line is fear of embarrassment or the repeat of success. It also comes with a twist. Going through Shot 6 can take *time*.

Quick basketball references here. We have all seen, and even laughed at someone who has taken a free throw in a basketball game, and it doesn't even hit the rim. It's a complete miss! And it happens to everyone, from amateurs to All-Stars. Jayson Tatum is one of my favorite NBA players, and while extremely successful, even he will have off-nights on the court. When that happens, you can tell *something* is *off.*

Shot 6 comes at the perfect time to "remind" you that while you made it through Shot 5, and are halfway to going 10 for 10, it's *only half way*, and you still have a long way to go. You have tasted success, but these are reminders in life that can be scary. They cause frustration and distract you from your Purpose.

One of the main causes of losing control is self created, being *overconfident.* It's natural as we are all human. You get that taste of success and begin to think you can rule the world. "I got my first commission check and I'm going to be a real estate mogul like Phil Dunphy!"

You probably know the symptoms of being overconfident. Skip a day at school. Sleep in an extra hour. Not return that phone call. Forget an appointment that's on your calendar. All of these are signs of being overconfident, creating the feeling of "*I deserve this*". But they can come with a consequence.

Another symptom is that you *miss* out on a client who used someone else for services instead of you. You *miss* a critical review of the upcoming exam. You *miss* a call from a peer, subordinate, or friend who was having a bad day at home or work, and you realize that you should have been there for them. All of these things can shake your confidence, and you realize that everything you have done to get to this point to build that foundation is being tested.

Overconfidence happens to all of us. We all take our eye off the ball! And we all cut corners from time to time. It's ok and it's part of the process. It's a little scary, yet controllable at the same time when you understand the lesson below. Some things, however, that happen to you are *out* of your control.

YOUR BROTHER HAS AN AORTIC DISSECTION

A few years ago, on Mother's day, late in the afternoon, I got a call that my brother had gone to the ER with extreme abdominal pain. He had just gotten done with dinner, and the pain was so sudden and severe that he didn't want to take any chances. He went to the local emergency room because the pain was unlike anything he had ever experienced, being a level 10. After some tests, and unclear of exactly what was going on, the pain subsided and the doctor said it was probably a gall or kidney stone, and was going to be able to go home soon.

My brother, who is extremely aware of his diet, medical history, etc., told the doctor he never had one of those, and based on what he knew of them this was something different. It had to be something else.

It was. The doctors ran another series of tests and indeed determined that an aneurysm was leaking and he was having an aortic dissection. There was no going home that night, instead, a first class ambulance ride to the best hospital in the region to see a specialist in this area.

They called it a "Triple-A," or Abdominal Aortic Aneurysm. I had no idea what the hell that was, but as I learned more, it scared the hell out of me. Not as much as my brother though. He had to go through a surgery that lasted for several hours. While nearly always fatal if not diagnosed in time, the surgery, if successful, has a great recovery rate, though a very long one that takes many weeks if not months.

I wasn't there for the surgery. My brother instead wanted me to come up toward the end of the time in the hospital so I could help him recover, as he was going to need assistance post surgery, which was going to be a couple of weeks. The real scary part was the night before the surgery. I couldn't imagine what was going through his mind, but in mine I wasn't sure if I would ever see him again. I called several people that I knew who were pastors of local churches for prayers. It didn't matter the denomination! All prayers count.

He survived the surgery!!

I remember that trip up to Boston, and the anxiety of what I was going to witness when I finally saw him. Again, I was scared. When I finally got in the hospital room, he gingerly got up, 30 pounds lighter, and gave me a hug. A hug of life.

He said "Let's get the fuck out of here."

I had *never* seen so many prescriptions! Managing the pills and the pain was a challenge, but nothing like the recovery itself. My brother was going to be OK, but this was a long road back. It was only amplified when every home health care professional that visited said, "You are lucky to be alive."

I spent two weeks with my brother and hardly had the time or bandwidth to do any work. We both wanted to get back in control and into the routine, and ulti-mately get back to work. I guess you could say we were *both* on the scary air ball shot. Not only was this a very scary point in his life, it created a situation where we both were starting over to some degree as we got back into the normal routines, mine being only a couple of weeks, his being more than a couple of months.

The scary air ball shot will take you out of the game and put you on the bench for a period of time. I needed to get back in the game.

I remember going back into the office after that time away, and I wasn't sure what to do. My *routine* was off. I needed something to take my mind off all of the recent events and feel like I could accomplish something. As I opened the door to the office, I saw the 3 long slim boxes of desks that had been bought a few weeks ago. They were still in the box because of the "assembly required" stamp. No one wanted to tackle putting them together, so I did.

The first one sucked, taking over three hours. But the second and third one went by much quicker, and when done, I felt that I had accomplished something, albeit small. I was back in the game.

DISTRACTIONS WILL HAPPEN

When you get *back* in the game, and you will, you will feel a bit disoriented and wonder where to start? What do you do first, after being distracted from your 10 for 10 experience?

Practice! That's the lesson of this shot. Remember your routine? Go back to that and all of the details. Re-engage yourself in them.

Distractions *will* happen when achieving your greater Purpose. These distractions can be influenced by your own actions, like overconfidence, or they can be outside your control, like a major health scare. But what *you do* when things happen to you is important! Your Purpose becomes even more powerful as you get back to your practice.

Maybe you had a family member who went through a tough time. Just like I did when my brother almost died. We are closer than ever as a result.

Maybe, *you* are going through something.

Purpose isn't what you do, your Purpose is what you do when things happen to you.

When you are ready to get back in the game, Practice, and all of the details that go with it, will be waiting for you. In my case, it was assembling three office desks.

shot seven
THE LUCKY BOUNCE

All good things take *time* to develop. I know I have made this point along the way, but achieving your Purpose is not easy or instantaneous. But the framework of 10 for 10 was created to help us understand it more easily. That's why you see the word *Purpose* in PowerPoint presentations. It's easy to say but not easy to understand. Unless you take the time going 10 for 10 to truly experience it, you may find yourself with a pile of self-help books that give you lists of things (tasks) to do that will make you successful, but still missing one thing that is truly for you. Purpose.

If only there was a little extra "light" here and there that could reinforce the efforts of 10 for 10. There is. It's called Luck.

That's what Shot 7 is. The Lucky Bounce shot. Everyone has had a little luck along the way, and there is nothing wrong with success that comes even when you didn't expect it, or feel like you deserved it.

It causes an emotion of exclaiming *"Wow!"* You are not sure how you got this success, but you take the win.

It's easy to recognize the lucky shot. We have all witnessed crazy moments in sports where the unthinkable happens, and you sit wide-eyed in amazement because you can't believe what you just saw.

You may remember the infamous chip that Tiger Woods made at the Masters in 2005 at the 16th hole. The chip hooked around the green, losing momentum but ever so slowly rolled, appeared to stop, and seemingly peered into the cup. It seemed like forever! And then, it finally dropped in! It's one of the most iconic shots in golf ever.

The result is *delayed*. You don't know right away if your efforts will pay off. Most times when you "take a shot" you know right away the outcome. But in the Lucky Bounce shot, you *don't* know right away. The lucky shot can happen in moments, or possibly take days or even months to happen.

We all have had those head-scratching moments after a *lucky* moment in our lives. It starts out by the emotion of *Wow!* Then followed by comments like *"Why did that happen?"* or *"I never win anything."* You excitedly take the fortuitous bounce and move on.

Whether you win or watch somebody else win, the lucky shot is probably the most identifiable shot in going 10 for 10, because everyone has that *Wow* moment collectively.

ENDING UP IN JACKSONVILLE

Years ago I lived in Merritt Island, Florida. Down by Cocoa Beach, the house I lived in had been newly built and had a pool. Bronson loved it and we got pretty good at playing frisbee as he would launch into the water to catch that floppy disc. It was a great location that included a commute, but I was overseeing restaurants from Orlando to Melbourne to Jacksonville, so it worked well enough.

On this particular beautiful sunny day in February, I was driving to Daytona to help wrap up Speed Week, which features the Daytona 500. It was a period of the busiest days and weeks of the year, and that one location was known for generating incredible sales that were counted on by the company.

I was still working for Hooters at the time. There were a ton of details to wrap up, though the staff and management were more than capable of working on these major events. I really was there as an extra set of hands, with no specific responsibilities for the day - merely to check in with the team and see where they needed help.

Heading north on I-95, it's a little over an hour to Daytona from Cocoa Beach. I really don't remember that drive much as I was tired myself, and I was either on the phone or listening to the radio. When I did remember and focus on what I was doing, I realized I had missed my exit. *By a lot!* When I got my bearings I realized it was about fifteen miles or so. Shit.

As I fumed at the road, it was a couple of miles to the next exit. This meant I would be driving an extra thirty miles and be 40 or so minutes later to Daytona than I wanted. Talk about screwing up. I had missed the exit (or the shot) and would have to turn around, start over and backtrack.

I started talking to myself. *"Do I really need to go to Daytona? There isn't anything specific I have to do there other than watch them clean up and finalize numbers. I've been there all week and it's not like they need me to do that."* Then I started thinking about when was the last time I was at some of the other restaurants and realized it had been a while since I had been to the one at the Jacksonville Landing. As the off ramp approached, I said out loud, *"To hell with Daytona. I'm going to Jacksonville."*

Another hour or so up the road and still irritated, I pulled into the parking garage and walked over to the restaurant in the quiet marketplace, as it was still morning and the retail shops and restaurants were preparing to open for the day. I said hi to the cooks prepping for lunch. I then walked into the office, and saw the general manager who was at the desk, doing some paperwork. As he made eye contact with me he had a look of amazement and asked, "What are *you* doing here? You are supposed to be in Daytona."

"I don't know. For some reason I ended up here, so let's have some fun." I don't really remember many details after that, as there was no agenda for the day other than taking a call from Daytona wondering where I

was. I don't even know what time I left to go home. But I *do* remember that surprised look on the general manager's face.

I do remember one other thing about that visit, but the memory didn't surface for several months.

Every summer there was a general manager conference, taking place around July. On the first night we were all at a cocktail reception and everyone was connecting and catching up. After a few beers, the general manager from Jacksonville approached me and asked for a moment. We grabbed another cold one and found an empty spot away from the group.

He said, "Remember that day you showed up at my store unannounced? You were supposed to be in Daytona."

"Yeah, I remember. Still not sure why that happened."

"Remember that I was doing paperwork?"

"I guess so. I remember more of how surprised you looked."

"That paperwork was my letter of resignation. I didn't feel like this was the place for me. But you showed up. And I didn't quit. Thank you."

He held up his beer and we clanked long necks.

Holy shit. *Wow!* I was blown away! I didn't have much to say other than you are welcome and thank you for telling me. That was certainly something he didn't have to do. I had no idea that the impact of my visit that day would be so significant, and it was a day that I would have probably forgotten forever. Now, I will never forget it.

In a way, I felt *lucky*, because if you have ever had someone quit under your leadership, it's frustrating on so many levels as you are losing a quality person, and having to hire and train someone new. It's so much more rewarding to train an employee to take a position, and when they are ready, promote him or her to a general manager to area supervisor. That's what happened several months later. That GM did get promoted, and in part because I was driving to Daytona and ended up in Jacksonville.

WINNING 50 BUCKS

I've never won the lottery, other than a free ticket here and there, but it's fun to buy that ticket, as you briefly think how you would handle winning a big jackpot, especially when they get over several millions of dollars.

I also like to give away scratch off lottery tickets, as it's fun to see the look in people's eyes as you can tell they are thinking for a brief moment what would happen if they won a big pay day. I normally never know if they won anything or not, but that's not the point. But one time, I did hear about a winner and again, it was a *wow* moment I will never forget.

I was running a Wednesday bi-weekly networking event that meets over lunch and I would give a door prize away in the form of a $5 scratch-off ticket. Thanks to beginner's luck, if you will, a lady and first-time attendee won the door prize. No one had ever met her before, but she was the winner and took the ticket. Meeting over.

The next day was Thursday, and I hosted the long-standing network event I've hosted for several years. That event was always better attended, with about fifty people. The meeting got underway, with people doing their 60-second introductions, and I noticed that the same lady from the previous day who won the scratch off ticket was there. It was nice that she decided to attend another event that I hosted, and I felt *lucky* that she was there, which added to the total weekly attendance.

After the meeting, there is usually a period where people will continue to network, exchange business cards, give referrals, set up one-to-one conversations over coffee, etc. This day was no exception, and the crowd hung around for about 20 minutes. I was putting my notes away and the new attendee, who won the scratch-off, came up to me.

"Thanks for hosting this event. I really enjoyed it. Do you remember me from the meeting yesterday? I won the lotto ticket."

"Yes! Glad you were able to make both events."

"I really want to thank you. That ticket was a winner. I won $50. When I visited your group yesterday, I wasn't sure why I was there. I do know that I had hardly any gas in the tank, and I wasn't sure how I was going to feed the kids when they got home. Your lotto ticket saved me."

Wow! I was speechless again. The simplicity of a small expense and gesture turned out to be a major event for someone. You never know what small actions today can lead to powerful results tomorrow.

We exchanged pleasantries, and I never saw her again.

NEXT THURSDAY IS RESERVED FOR "THE MAN!"

I was still early in the real estate phase of my life, now past the memory of my first closing. While gaining momentum, there still was plenty of room for improvement. I was going to a lot of networking groups, up to five or six per week, and meeting as many people as I could to grow my list of professional connections.

One of the individuals I met was a man named Scott. He was a sales coach, with a solid business, and he was well-known for hosting networking events and being on the board of the Marietta Business Association. He had a strong, yet encouraging, personality and I always enjoyed talking to him casually. For some reason I never approached him for help on sales, probably because I assumed he was going to cost more than my budget would allow, and I didn't want to waste his time.

I remember one afternoon at the weekly networking meeting, Scott announced that he was going to start a new networking group at his church, and that he would be stepping away from this group for some time while he developed that. I went up to him and said congratulations and he pulled me aside.

He said, "I've been watching you grow. You are doing all the right things! Keep doing them, and I would be honored if you would check out this new group to support its growth."

I was super excited! I was *asked* by this superstar, in my opinion, to be a part of his group. I attended and, while it was small at first, it grew to a healthy size and I met a new group of great professionals. I felt lucky to be a part of something new.

About a month went by in this new group and again, Scott came up to me and was excited about my growth and success. Finally, I asked him if I could meet him for breakfast or lunch one day for some coaching or advice. He said absolutely and to send him an email. Again, I felt lucky.

I sent that email on Friday morning to ask him to meet and he responded, "Next Thursday am is reserved for THE MAN!! What time and where, my partner?"

I still have that email and that response is word for word.

Scott died on Sunday.

The crazy thing was that no one in the Marietta Business Association, where he was a board member, (that's how I had met him), knew about it. Why would they? Scott had been on a personal trip, and his church found out first as that was closer to his family. Scott had kept two circles of people in his life, professional and personal, with little crossover.

Months earlier, I had sent out postcards to various neighborhoods for marketing Purposes, hoping for a call that would generate a lead. By "luck" one those postcards became the key to connecting those two circles.

I got the call that Sunday night. It was from one of the aldermen at the church. The alderman was responsible for letting key people in his life know what happened. As the members of the church put together the pieces of whom to call and how to connect with them, my name came up as a possible connection. Simultaneously, when my name was mentioned to the alderman, he said, "I know that guy. His picture has been on my fridge for six months!"

It was one of my postcards that enabled us to connect. Talk about luck!

Even though I never got to meet Scott to learn how I may be able to grow my business, it grew regardless. I kept going to that networking group, in part to help those that knew him well grieve, and in part to keep my commitment that I had made to Scott when he asked me to participate. You never know how going 10 for 10 will be supported through unlikely circles and connections!

Is it possible to create your own "luck" through hard work? While obviously losing Scott was terrible and challenging to many, finding positive outlooks is another key part of actualizing your 10 for 10 journey, and of course, your Purpose.

THE HARDER YOU WORK, THE LUCKIER YOU GET

The lucky shot is absolutely an accomplishment, which is the lesson here. Going back to the old video of that high school basketball game when I went 10 for 10, I watched all 10 of those made free throws. There was one where I released the ball and lost my balance. It was painful to watch! But it went in the basket somehow.

No matter how awkward the shot looks, or feels, it counts the same. I couldn't have made all 10 free throws if that one didn't go in. And when you are going 10 for 10, there will be at times an experience that doesn't feel like a success immediately, but with a little luck it does. The delayed response counts, and it actually creates memories you think of for a long time.

It doesn't have to be a lucky chip shot at the Masters that hangs on the lip of the cup until gravity tugs it in. It could be a simple act that your gut tells you to do at that moment.

Just like the time I decided to keep driving up that highway. The moment I chose to keep going and not turn around was awkward, but it felt like the right thing to do.

Just like the time when I gave the lottery ticket to the woman at the networking event whom no one had previously ever met. I suppose everyone, including her, would have been fine with drawing another name since she had just stumbled awkwardly into the group, but it felt like the right thing to do.

Just like I did when my friend Scott died. My actions of staying involved with that group has brought business and the person who called me that night, because he had my postcard, still gives me referrals to this day.

When you embrace the power of the lucky shot, just accept the win. Your actions may feel awkward, but know that there is an accomplishment coming. It may take time of course, but if your gut is telling you something, listen to it.

Going 10 for 10 is a powerful experience, and as you begin to look at the latter shots, you should feel the building momentum of this journey. The made shots are more impactful, and yet, the missed ones have more consequences.

Remember the momentum of the confidence from the accomplishments you made in Shot 5? That will carry you through the emotions of accepting the accomplishments that everyone screams "Wow! You got lucky!"

shot eight
KICK IN THE ASS

The miss of the K.I.T.A. shot, or *Kick In The Ass*, represents events in your life that are true setbacks. They sting hard. They will humble you, and force you to think about your actions that took you here, and what corrections you need to make. The actions may be obvious to spot. The corrections though can live in your subconscious. And the thing that sucks the most about the K.I.T.A. shot? *Time.*

How can something that appears so close be so far away? When you get to shot 8, you are so close to the finish line of 10 for 10. It's just two more shots after this one to achieve that 10 for 10 moment and fulfill your Purpose. But Shot 8 will fool you, because when you take this shot, there *will* be a miss. Shot 3, which seems so long ago, may have led to an initial feeling of frustration and disappointment. But now, in Shot 8, you just want to quit.

Here's what a K.I.T.A looks like:

- ► You are passed over for the job you were told was earmarked for you. Then you find out it went to a peer with less experience instead.

- ► Your girlfriend or boyfriend breaks up with you.

- ► Your spouse says they want a divorce.

- ► You get fired from your job. Call it furloughed, company reorganization, etc. It's all the same shit and *it sucks.*

- ► You get into an accident from a car, a fall, etc. that puts you in the emergency room.

- ► You hang out with the wrong group of people, get in trouble with the police, and go to jail.

- ► You lose out on a big sale that you needed to close to pay the bills.

You get the idea, and probably already are thinking of one that's happened to you. They can happen in a split second, yet the time you are forced to take to recover may seem like an eternity. In that moment, you experience the rage, sadness, despair, and anxiety created by any of those instances listed above.

Unlike many of the other shots, you don't get to go back to the line right away. There is too much to deal with. And if you rush back too quickly, you set yourself up to miss the KITA shot *again*. Think of it like an NFL star that tears their ACL and tries to play the next week. We all know that will result in more pain, more damage, and even longer to heal.

Overcoming adversity is a life skill that can't be taught, it can only be experienced. But I can tell you stories that may resonate with you. Adversity is universal, bouncing back is critical, especially when the adversity *really freakin' sucks*. Shot 8 is by far the hardest shot you will ever take in your life. Because you will miss it. Maybe multiple times. That's why it's called a Kick In The Ass!

YOU'RE FIRED

Here's what it looked like for me. I was a Divisional Vice President at Hooters, the best job I ever had. The phone rang all the time recruiting me to other opportunities and I always declined, thinking that the job would last forever. My ridiculous belief failed to acknowledge the pending changes in the organization, so I kept doing the same thing in my job. And then one day we were all called to a reorganization meeting and had to "re-interview" for a new position. I got a different title with similar wages and thought everything was great for a couple of weeks, until my boss called me to meet for a beer.

"You're fired."

I was pissed. I cried. I was alone. My wife at the time was even too busy to meet me because she was out with friends. That pissed me off even more. And similar to Shot 5 when you experience the silent win, *no one* called me with condolences after this loud loss. Someone once told me that you learn who your friends really are in situations like this, and I never understood that until this point.

Just like that, I was erased from the company I spent over ten years with. Immediately, I was looking for a new job, and called all my contacts, thinking that surely I would have a new job immediately. In the meantime, the emotions turned from being mad to being scared of what I was going to do next, to being embarrassed as I had to tell everyone that I was unemployed.

I got a new job within a few weeks. It was similar in nature to my role at Hooters, with a little more control with less resources. It paid well, and I was right back to the line breezing through 10 for 10! Within a few months, I was on Shot 5, as the confidence and bank account were rocking once again.

Two years later I was back at Shot 8, and missed again. That job didn't work out either.

As I look back at that experience, I wonder if things would have been different had I taken more *time* to pause and think about what I wanted from the new job. What if I had taken more time to find the right resources? Maybe, at an even more basic level, even thought about what I wanted out of my entire career altogether?

I also wonder, even before the reorganization, *what if I had stopped while I was in my position to recognize the changes coming? Could I have done anything different to prevent it from happening?* Would I have made Shot 8 if I had paused for a little longer before I took it?

The K.I.T.A. forces you to think. Do you remain on the same path you were on because you are confident you can get past Shot 8, or do you stay the course because you are scared of charting a new path? The K.I.T.A. is real shit.

$9,660

We all have little souvenirs in our homes, offices, garages, etc. that are a gift, a symbol, or note that reminds of past experiences. Some are more important than others, of course, and as you look around your desk, you can easily identify them. But if someone else were to put eyes on it, it might not be so obvious, unless you tell the backstory to shed light. On my desk, there is a piece of paper from a Levenger notepad (fancy corporate notepad) that says $9660. It was one of my favorite K.I.T.A.'s.

I had gotten the real estate license and was practicing it part-time, with the intent one day to do it full time. Easier said than done, as doing a job as a 1099 full commission independent contractor is *very* different from a full-time W2 employee, who is expected to produce results for a full-time salary.

I had done some real estate work and attended some meetings and appointments in the broker's office, but it was part-time and sporadic, because the corporate job had to take precedence. I wasn't really growing the real estate business, because I was obligated to my position as the restaurant's director of operations and wanted to make sure I was committed to that first. Through my hopes and dreams, I would have enough saved to make the switch, or even better, make enough "side" money in real estate that would put me "over the top" financially, if you will. In the meantime, the corporate job required extensive travel, about 70% of the time, preventing me from really spending any quality time to effectively make that transition.

I did begin to make some contacts that I thought had promise. One of those contacts was a friend who wanted to buy a house as they were renting and said they would be happy if I could help them with the purchase when the time was right.

Here we go! I was going in the right direction and this was the beginning of big things. Until it wasn't. I didn't follow up. I just assumed I would get the call when the time was right. I did get the call, but not the one I expected. I was on a plane after being out of town for several days of work and the call came in as I was landing.

"Hey are you in town? If so, do you want to have a steak and some beer?"

That sounded good to me. I was ready to be done with work for the week. I replied that it sounded awesome. He would get the steak and I would bring the beer.

"I will text you my address." I knew where he lived so that was irrelevant.

"We just bought a house." *That* was relevant. My heart sank.

As I drove to the new house with a twelve-pack of beer, my mind went into "what the fuck?" mode. How was this possible, and why didn't I get the call to help buy this house? When I got the tour of the gorgeous new home, I finally asked the question after a couple of beers.

"If you don't mind, I thought I was going to be involved in this process. What happened?"

"Yeah, we are sorry about that. This all happened so quickly and we had to move on it fast. We didn't want to bother you because we knew you were too busy." They ended up using another broker that did real estate full-time and was available. I was not.

Too...busy.

As I drove home, my emotions were all over the board as you can imagine. I was pissed off. I was mad, and I had no words, or at least not any positive ones. I remember the first thing I did when I got home. I went to my computer, logged on to the MLS (Multiple Listing Service) program I belonged to, and looked up that house. I looked at the sale price, grabbed a calculator, did the quick math of what my split would have been after I paid the marketing fee and broker split. The total net commission was $9,660.

Talk about a Kick In The Ass! This was a complete miss on my part. I wanted to blame so many people! However, the only person I could blame was me. I knew I had to make some changes in my life, as my Purpose was off. My *behavior* was off. I had taken for granted that I could just do my existing job for the restaurant while also being successful in what I really wanted to do. It was not an automatic slam dunk.

All behavior, in fact, is Purposeful. I had to learn and remember how 10 for 10 works. Only *you* can take the shot. So if it's a miss, it's on you. In this case, *Me*.

FORK IN THE ROAD

Sorry, my reader, let me pour you a shot here, because you will miss this shot at some point. Why? because 10 for 10 is how you live your life, and we are not all perfect. The familiar term *"failing forward"* can apply here, because some of the greatest lessons in your life happen because of failure, and that may have happened to you as you think about Shot 8, or maybe it's yet to come. *Maybe* you are shot 8 *right now*.

Hence the fork in the road. The K.I.T.A. gives you a choice to make as you go back to the beginning. Do you do the *same* thing again? Or do you do something *different?* Maybe it's the exact same job title. Maybe it's a different type of job. Maybe it's a new profession altogether. Maybe it's going from a 1099 job to a W-2 job, or vice versa.

Regardless, tomorrow will look differently than today once you experience a K.I.T.A. And if you don't take the time to think about the *fork in the road*, this shot will be a *roadblock* again at some point.

In my case, I knew to *change my future*, and to be successful selling real estate, I would have to act like a professional in the industry and do it full-time. If I didn't I would never make it past this shot, which meant I would have to sacrifice something major, which was my current job with a guaranteed paycheck.

The more time I spend talking about Purpose, going 10 for 10, and this shot in particular, *everyone* has had a K.I.T.A. that they are dealing with. I think that what makes going 10 for 10 so powerful is that even though it's just you on the line, everyone is on the line at some point. When you take the time to check yourself, you learn that there are people to help you. As you experience the process of repeating the shots, you also recognize that you are one of those people helping others get past this shot.

I think about that first closing I had when I helped finish loading up the moving truck. Were my clients experiencing a K.I.T.A. of some sort? What about that general manager in Jacksonville? He was writing his resignation letter when I visited. Was he experiencing a K.I.T.A.? Surely, my brother was. Hell, he didn't know if he was going to live.

All of these lessons taught along the way to go 10 for 10 are about to pay off. It's one thing to be taught a lesson. The power is internalizing it.

PROCESSING THE NEXT SHOT

Do you recognize a K.I.T.A from any of the examples above? Girlfriend breaking up with you? Was it totally on her? Fired from your job completely due to un-reasonable expectations from your boss? Was the speeding ticket because of a cop on a power trip? I can't think of *any* KITA shot I have missed over the years that wasn't a result of my behavior in some way, shape, or form.

I bet you can't either. Take some *time* and think about that.

I bet you can remember similar events of other people's behavior too, where a setback or mistake was solely due to someone else. Blaming others for our own circumstances tends to make matters worse. Before we go back to the line, we have to reflect on why we missed Shot 8. We have to own the misses, as well as the makes, and the lesson learned clicks: *Promise.*

Ah- our old friend Promise, whom we haven't seen since Shot 3, the What the Hell shot. Think back to the significance of promise. In order for a promise to be kept, you have to make a sacrifice. Speaking of "what the hell" *you already* know what the promise is and the sacrifice it will take to get back to this shot and make it. And it *scares the hell out of you.*

You have to feel the pain of the miss in order to understand how to push forward to Shots 9 and 10. The old adage goes, "Without pain, how could we feel joy?"

Pausing to think about all of your actions on this shot, how you got here, and why you missed is critical. By taking the time, you can fully process your actions, your desired results, and how it affects others as well.

This journey may seem endless, and it may even make you give up hope. Just remember Shot 1: "Hopes and Dreams." If you really make a Promise to yourself to follow the process of 10 for 10, you *will* make it past this shot.

I promise.

shot nine
THE PRESSURE COOKER

When you get this far along in your 10 for 10 journey, you reach this point and there's a different feeling: *you want the ball.* You have no reservations about taking the shot, because you have put in the time. You have gone through all of the emotions. And yes, you have put in the *practice.*

Have you ever seen the look in someone's eyes when they are truly in the zone? They almost look like they are in a different universe. Those intense glares of focus. The internal voice that tells you to just stay out of the way because they are going to get the job done. The pressure is high, but so is your mental toughness when you are in the zone.

Something begins to evolve as your confidence grows to a level that you haven't thought about much. Credibility. Your credibility is beginning to evolve in a way you may not yet be able to explain, but think about that for a second. Your confidence now is much stronger than it was in Shot 5, the Confidence shot. The fact that you *want* the ball is powerful. It's not because you want to be the center of attention. It's because you *know* you can deliver results for others when they are counting on you.

That's what drives me every time I get the opportunity to speak in front of groups to talk about Purpose, and 10 for 10. While I'm the one on stage, it's not about me. It has to be about you. Otherwise, I am just being selfish, throwing the frisbee, and not caring who is there to catch it.

When you experience this shot, indeed your credibility is taking form.

The Pressure Cooker shots are so intense that there are only a few people that can make them based on the situation, and when those situations arise, it becomes pretty clear that the person who has put in the time, the practice, the promise, and has experienced the accomplishments is the one who will take the shot.

The different feeling that you get now, *wanting the ball,* is the result of putting in all of the hard work along the way. For me, at least in part, it was to prove to all of the doubters that I could get this far. I guess that stems all the way back to those high school days when Coach said I probably would never play. Those were the roots of the pressure, way back then! His honesty was sincere, but the doubt was too. It was up to me to prove to everyone, including myself, that I could achieve great things.

When I take this shot, I know others are counting

on me, such as all of my clients who have gone to the closing table with the desire of walking away with keys or cash from buying or selling a house.

By the way, you won't miss this shot. You have gone all in on the framework of 10 for 10, and it's time to wipe the sweat from your brow, take the ball, and show everyone that your Purpose is powerful!

NURSE NANCY

I was the general manager of a Mexican Restaurant called Margaritas in East Hartford, Connecticut. This was a very popular regional chain in New England, and without a doubt was a destination for both families and bar goers as it had a dedicated dining room and bar area. Friday nights were heavily focused on the bar sales, and Saturday nights would trend toward the families in the dining room, many with parties of six guests or more.

Those who have worked in a restaurant know that there are certain key positions. In my mind, one of those is the host, because they control who sits where and when. It's a big puzzle and if the hostess screws up the floor chart, you are in for a very long night. Another is the dishwasher. They get no credit and are always covered in shit. It's a tough job that seemingly never ends until that last pot is scrubbed, the floor is mopped, and trash cued for the back door. Back in the day when paychecks were actually physical pieces of paper that were hand delivered, I made it a point to physically hand them to the dishwashers first. They deserved it along with the handshake of appreciation.

Obviously, the cook line is essential, as that's where the meals are prepared. But there is one more line, and that is the expo line. The expo line is a very simple concept, as it's where all of the plates of food are assembled, garnished and placed in order so the servers can deliver them to the guests. While it's simple when there is just a table or two of orders, it's chaotic when there is a full house of guests. It's like putting dozens of puzzles together at once. During the dinner rush, this high-stakes game never lets up, lasting for two hours at a time.

I've seen a lot of people who claim that they are good at expo. I've also seen a lot of people who struggle at expo too, because expo is the pressure cooker shot. You need the person on expo to say "Give me the damn ball," because that person knows how to thrive under pressure when you are serving a couple of hundred meals on a Saturday night.

How hard can it be? What could go wrong? Everything. If you don't have a complete team that understands their role, from the host who properly seats the dining room, to the manager that informs the kitchen how many menus are on the tables to indicate how many meals are soon to be cooked, to the servers alerting the manager of orders of long cook times coming (like a well done steak), to the expo person themselves, preparing the line to get the food out in a timely and proper manner, you have all the perfect ingredients to prepare a classic *shit show.*

Send out the wrong item to one table? Wrong. You have sent out the wrong item to *two tables,* at least. Now you have to redo the order, which slows down everyone behind it. Add in some upset servers, a cook who messes up an order, etc., and you have a real fun time on your hands! God bless the expo person for making it all happen.

Fortunately on this night, it was *smooth.* Very few issues, with a packed house on a Saturday night. Everyone was pumped up, because when all the engines are firing in a busy restaurant, everyone is happy, from the servers who are making great tips, to the customers who can't wait to come back, to the cooks, who want to ask for a raise.

Everything was great. Until the Front of House Manager said "Brent, we have a problem." I looked at the amount of orders yet to be cooked and it was less than 5-6.

"What do you mean, *we* have a problem"?

"It's Table 63. A single top."

"Where the hell is Table 63?? That's not even on our seating chart?"

"Well it is. Sort of. It's a small table by the bathroom, next to the statue with the big smiling sun, used to roll silverware. The hostess sat her there, no one waited on her and it took over an hour for her to get her food after she asked someone for help."

That sun statue was smiling with a shit eating grin. I was not.

"Well, why didn't you handle it?"

"Because I think you probably are the only one that *can* handle it."

Give me the damn ball.

I walked over to the now infamous Table 63, and there she was, the woman sitting by herself. She had been in the restaurant before and had always sat by herself, usually reading a book while she ate. As I sat down at her table, I immediately said hello, my name is Brent, the general manager, and I know I have a big apology coming your way. She calmly replied that she knew who I was, her name was "Nancy."

I told her that her meal was on me and that this delay in service would not happen again. But what she said next I will never forget.

"I am a nurse, and work in the emergency room to help people who are hurt. Some people are hurt very badly, and are in there for various reasons. Some had bad things happen to them, and some were hurt because they tried to do bad things to other people. Those people who caused harm to others, I would love to just pass by their room and not help them. But I don't get to choose. We don't have sections like your servers do, and we have to help *everyone*."

I instantly could feel a large lump develop in my throat, and my forehead could feel the sweat building. I knew where she was going with this, but I knew I had to let her finish her point, which was that every server that worked in the dining room had a choice as they walked by her several times. They could have easily acknowledged her even though she wasn't in their assigned section. Instead, they chose to ignore her, and by the time someone did choose to address her, the damage was done. We had served over 200 people that night, but one person was ignored in such a fashion that the whole night felt like a failure. This was unacceptable.

This could have been a situation that I just bought her meal, thanked her and made a note about it to make sure she got better service. Yet this was a Pressure Cooker situation, and more needed to be done to ease the pressure.

I immediately changed our systems to address this. This included additional host training that mandated any solo diner was personally brought to the manager on duty's attention. The manager would promptly greet the guest in person, and make sure the server knew too. I also made sure that their meal was pushed through ahead of all other meal orders so their wait was not long since they were dining solo.

The pressure of the Nurse Nancy story is two-fold. The first part was that agonizing approach to her and listening to her story, talking to her, and trying to

THE POINT IS IN THE PURPOSE

make her feel that we would solve her problem. The second part was actually solving it.

I think Nurse Nancy wanted me to know that day that it's one thing to dress a wound. It's another thing to make sure the wound properly heals!

PRACTICE TAKES PATIENCE

When I was a kid, I remember my parents making me go to bed around 7:30 p.m. or so. That sucked, because it was still early and I didn't want to go to bed. And in the spring, it was still light out. Why the hell would you go to bed when it was still light out? I would turn on my radio softly to listen to the Red Sox play-by-play until I gradually fell asleep.

As I'm older now, I would *gladly* go to bed as early as possible so I can get ready for the next day and catch up on sleep. I think that this probably applies to every kid who wishes to stay up until the end of the ballgame, and adults who look forward to going to bed.

Practice makes perfect, so they say.

What's the lesson you truly learn on the Pressure Cooker shot? *Practice.*

We've been over this before, of course. You learn how important practice is when you develop a routine. You understand how critical practice is when scary shit happens in your life. Of course, that doesn't mean you look forward to practice, though. Practice is hard.

166

It takes time. It takes repetition. And it takes patience. All of these things lead to accomplishments!

Shot 4 is Routine right? You need to practice. And what happens? Shot 5. Confidence, because of the accomplishments resulting from that practice.

Same thing in Shot 6. It's a scary shot. But you focus on the practice. And what happens? Shot 7. It's Lucky because of an accomplishment.

You *can't* have accomplishments without *practice!*

That's why repetition is so important. The process of 10 for 10 illustrates how the repetition of practicing free throw after free throw ties into all of the experiences you live in life to achieve your Purpose.

And just like that young child who didn't want to go to bed is like that younger version of yourself that didn't *want* to practice, the older version of yourself who can't wait to go to bed at night *craves* practice.

I realized that by crushing my regular routine, I would be ready for the Pressure Cooker shot when someone handed me the ball, or in impromptu moments, like the time I met Nurse Nancy. All of this practice pays off, and you can't wait to get to practice. The lessons taught in practice are finally internalized. Selfishness is not a good attribute, but I think it's OK to be selfish about your practice. The more time you spend on *you and your practice* benefits you and everyone around you.

I have never missed the Pressure Cooker shot. Too much is on the line, and whatever practice I need to do to make this shot I will do it.

You won't miss it either, as *long* as you've put in the practice!

shot ten
THE MONEY SHOT

There are no surprises here on shot 10. No funny bounces, no traps, no airballs. Just "game-winning" shots that seal the deal for you in going 10 or 10. The Money shot represents incredible moments in your life. You will never forget them, as these are your "15 minutes of fame," like going 10 for 10 in a state semifinal.

Take the time to reflect on those moments, regardless of your age, and celebrate them. We certainly remember the major *misses* in life, so make sure you remember the quality wins too. I had buried the 10 for 10 basketball game because I was supposed to "live life" after high school, but this moment has been so much more powerful by keeping it front in center. It became the backbone of Purpose.

You may find though, that there really aren't a lot of these big moments. *That's* what makes going 10 for 10 so powerful. There may not be a ton of 10 for 10 moments or achievements, but they define you. It's *your Purpose.* In Fact, *that's the point in the Purpose. Going 10 for 10.*

The average person lives about 77.5 years. That's 22,287.5 days. If I asked you to remember 22,287 moments, good or bad, in your life, that's tough to do. But what about *ten* moments in your life that you will never forget? Maybe that's receiving a perfect score on an important exam in high school. Or receiving acceptance into a college. Earning a scholarship to play your favorite sport. Meeting your spouse for the first time and knowing in that moment you'd be together forever. Getting married. Your first *major* promotion. The birth of your children. Retirement. A fifty-year wedding anniversary. Attending the funeral of your spouse, and while sad, being so thankful for everything you achieved with them.

All of these Money shots represent major achievements in your life, and yet they all are wrapped up with lessons you learn by keeping promises, practicing your skills, and accomplishing milestones along the way. Additionally, the Money shots pay homage to your failures along the way too.

Going 10 for 10 is not easy. There is nothing easy about getting a perfect score on that final exam in high school. You had to study. Nothing easy about getting into college. Nothing easy about getting a scholarship. You had to *practice.* Nothing easy about being married. You have to *promise.* Nothing easy about getting that major promotion. You had to have *accomplishments.* Nothing easy about raising children. Staying married. Staying fulfilled after retirement. And there is nothing easy about coming home from a funeral wondering how you will start a new chapter in life, even though you don't want to.

And as I say that 10 for 10 is not easy, remember; It's not *supposed to be easy.*

Can you identify *ten unforgettable* times in your life that helped you achieve your greater Purpose?

Finish your drink. I will go first.

1. ***The 10 for 10 game in high school***—That game for me was my 15 minutes of fame, and it has become the center of everything I reflect on in the framework of achieving your Purpose. Thank you to my coach and teammates for providing me that experience!

2. ***Dad handing me my high school diploma***—My father was my principal and while a major accomplishment, I reflect on the crazy highs and lows of being the son of the principal. It's helped me stay balanced with all of the "missed" shots along the way. Thanks Dad!

3. ***My brother survived an aortic dissection***—That was one of the scariest times in my life, and I didn't even experience it firsthand. I remember sitting on the "T" in Boston going to the hospital

to pick up my brother. That time of silence on the train to the point of entry into the hospital room where my brother gave me that hug of life knowing that he would be OK was something I will never forget. So glad to have you as my brother Marc!

4. **Being promoted to a Divisional Vice President at Hooters**—That accomplishment is something that I am very proud to have experienced. Thank you to all those who shaped one of the best parts of my career!

5. **My Mom, for teaching me the art of teaching the transfer**—Presenting information to a large group is one thing. Keeping them engaged is another. There is an art to "teaching the transfer" as you move from one point to another to properly illustrate your overall message. It was an eye-opening lesson for me to help me with my presentation skills. It's something I continue to practice. Thanks Mom!

6. **Being the President of the Marietta Business Association**—Business associations are very popular in Cobb County, Georgia, and I was fortunate to be the Marietta president for one year. The theme? *Purpose,* of course! That experience has given me the continued

opportunity to host one of the more popular networking events in the area, serve as a board member on another business association in Kennesaw, and it's been a springboard for my speaking opportunities. Thanks to the over 20,000 people who have attended those networking events!

7. ***Sunsets on the Pacific Coast beaches in Central America and Moons in Alaska*** –Awe-inspiring sights like these have created everlasting impressions for me that shed light on dark days. Whether a full moon rising on a clear, cold night in February in Alaska, or a giant ball of fire falling into the Pacific with a surfer gliding off one last wave to shore, those memories make happy hour that much better. Pour me a tall one, bartender!

8. ***Celebrating over 10 years of selling real estate full time, and making a living doing it*** –I'm still here to help you and your friends make wise decisions. Thank you to all of my clients in the past, present, and those I've yet to meet. Thank you also to my closest friends who have never wavered in their support!

9. ***Writing this book*** –Going through all of these shots in print to give you the reader something

173

tangible has been an amazing experience and I can tell you I have experienced *all* of the emotions, success, and misses of every shot while going through this process. From the Hopes and Dreams of just wanting to have a chance to do this, to the Good Luck looks and vibes from others at networking events when explaining the book concept early on, to the Confidence of getting the first few pages edited, to the KITA of wanting to quit, and to the Pressure of just keep going, I've felt it all. Thank you to my team of friends and professionals that kept me on track!

10. **Bronson**—Now gone almost as long as he was alive, I think of that dog, my best friend, every day. Without Bronson I never would have thrown that damn frisbee 10,000 times and, without that daily routine of being with my dog, I never would have learned how to identify Purpose. Thank you, my grey ghost friend.

NOW IT'S YOUR TURN

I love telling stories, as you can tell. That's what "bartenders" do. But while in part the stories are designed to entertain, they also are there so you can put them into perspective around your own situation. Maybe the stories are just to entertain, but maybe some of them resonate with you, or even teach you something, inspiring you to act on it.

That's what 10 for 10 is designed to do. So as your favorite bartender announces that last call is coming in a couple minutes, it's your turn to grab that cocktail napkin and jot down some notes of your own:

My Purpose is:

I'm on Shot #:

The 10 things I'm most proud of are:

I wonder how your list looks! Ironically, none of mine referenced any specific amount of money. For sure, I have made money along the way. We all have. But when I look back at specific amounts of money, like my first commission check when I started selling real estate, they always fall into Shot 5. They are accomplishments, but for me they just give me confidence to keep working at what I like to do so that others want to participate. Money is important, and we all need it. Your Purpose, though, ultimately provides renewal. Don't forget that.

Also, here's *your* check. Don't forget to tip your bartender!

REFLECTING ON THE MAKES AND MISSES

As you work that list of the ten milestones above, you have learned how powerful accomplishments are. You know how the Purpose process works, and you have a road map. You know how to Define your Purpose. You know how to Identify your Purpose, and you know how to Achieve it. You know what the emotions and lessons of each shot are, so you can maximize the gains and minimize the losses.

In your life journey, you will *make* and *miss* a lot of shots. That's OK. It's not considered a journey otherwise. Everyone has makes and misses in life just like you. But you understand something now many people don't.

Purpose.

My Purpose is to help you and your friends make wise decisions that produce favorable results.

Perhaps you, the reader, live a life with a strong understanding of your Purpose. Hopefully this gives you a perspective to enhance yours.

Maybe, you the reader, had little or no idea what your Purpose was. Hopefully this gives you that road map you have been searching for!

Wherever you are, remember that when you achieve your Purpose, you also are helping someone along the way achieve theirs, *even* if they don't know the language of 10 for 10.

Finally, the dirty, little secret is that the journey to 10 for 10 never actually stops. For me, even after milestones like graduating high school, being promoted to Divisional Vice President, celebrating a decade of selling real estate, and going 10 for 10, the next journey was waiting. The same will be the case for you as you go 10 for 10.

I guess that marks the last call for the night.

ONE FINAL SHOT

T hanks for taking some time to check out the book. Hopefully there was a takeaway—or 10—that will give you some help to define, identify, and achieve your Purpose. Ever since I started talking publicly about Purpose and 10 for 10, the number one question I was asked was "Do you have a book?" My answer was no. I didn't think I needed one.

I just kept working on developing my keynote, the 10 for 10 registered trademark, the merchandise, website, doing podcasts, and speaking wherever I could. And every time the conversation came up, the "where's the book?" comment would resurface.

I started asking the question back. "Do you think I need a book?" I started hearing yes, because it would help my business. Maybe it will. But when I started hearing yes, it was because people began telling me that they doubted their Purpose too. They needed to hear my stories.

I guess I needed to hear them too. It's taken over two years from the time I created an outline to the time I found the perfect publisher for me who could guide me through the process and teach me how to write. *Most Important:* Never once did I use an AI platform to write for me, even though every time I would look at a blank docs screen a "help me write" prompt would pop up. I was not going there, and if the words you have read at times felt unpolished or raw, they were my words, not Gemini's or Copilot's or whatever GPT. And while there is nothing wrong with the evolution of technology, this was not the time or place for me.

The other thing I wanted, and needed to do was weave the stories into the lessons that made sense, hence the reference to the bartender. A good bartender is busy with many guests but keeps you engaged, even if he steps aside to do another task or help another guest. But he always controls the narrative of the experience, drink after drink. I have always been the person who would rather pour you the drink vs. order it, and again, thanks to my editor, Andrew brought that natural style into my writing.

A good bartender can also tell stories that they were not necessarily a part of, and that includes your stories. I want and need to hear your stories too! If you want to tell me yours, send me an email to Brent@10for10.net and maybe it will show up in a newsletter, or even be featured at an upcoming presentation. Or if you want to have me speak to your group, let's connect!

As you close this book and throw it in the pile of others on your shelf, you may be asking a simple question now that you know how to go 10 for 10:

"Can I make 11?"

Cheers to Your Purpose!

ACKNOWLEDGEMENTS

If going 10 for 10 seems hard, trying to thank everyone who inspired me, supported me, and guided me through the process of writing (or even starting to write) *The Point is in the Purpose* is indeed a challenge. Let's give it a shot though (pun intended).

Thanks to Joe Kim for pulling out his camera one day and saying, "Stop talking about 10 for 10 and let's start videoing it." Thanks, Joe, for finding local places to test the concept of 10 for 10 and recording all my talks and one-minute videos. You deserve so much credit.

Thanks to Keith Ivey for encouraging me to facilitate groups and be my right-hand man at networking groups and large presentations. The first networking group I went to, Keith, was hosting, and I remember thinking, *I want to do that.* Keith taught me and I thank you!

Thanks to Dave Young for his never-ending support, willingness to write the foreword in this book, and for always saying yes to whatever help I needed. Dave easily could have said no as he had a young family, was starting a new business and serving his country, yet he always took the time to say yes.

Thanks to Megan Amodio for all the support and feedback with the keynote speech. I continuously work on perfecting the speech, and Megan has always been able to offer suggestions that make the message more powerful, and provide perspective on how the message is received by an audience.

Thank you to so many of my others who encouraged me to write, checked in along the way, and helped with the concept of branding, photography, book outlines, speech rehearsals, and friendship in general, including Jeff Bowman, Sheryl Lanham, Ferrell Middleton, David Clarke, Patti Willig, Justin Arndt, Bart Nunley, Jim Beach, and Greg Fuller.

Family is important and I am so fortunate to be part of several families. That's where the stories come from! Thank you to my Networking Opportunity Family! It has been a constant in my life every Thursday for over a decade, and I've met so many incredible people. Thank you, Michelle Garland, for being my Co-Host and helping with my Run of Show at local events! Thank you to my Marietta Business Association family! Thank you, Angella Ocheltree, Julie Michaels, and John Silvey, for believing in me. Thank you to my Kennesaw Business Association family! Thanks to Marlon Longacre for mentoring how a Business Association works, and Ollie Patterson for his nonstop encouragement and keeping me "mic'd" up too! Thank you JRM management for your support of whatever I needed too.

Thank you to my original 10 for 10 family, the members of my High School Basketball team in Rockland Maine from 1985-86, including Coach Dave Cook, Chris Carpenter, and Peter Merriam. Thanks to all the stars on the team who allowed me to be the backup; the impact of the story wouldn't ever have surfaced otherwise.

Thank you to my Hooters Family, who taught me so many lessons and gave me so many experiences to remember. Thank you, along with countless others, Steve King, Marty Fayette, Bill Gowanloch, Tad Dixon, and Rick Akam.

Thank you to my family of Real Estate at High Caliber Realty. Bill Borden, Brenda Bordan, and Steve Hale have been so supportive in growing my Real Estate business and I am thankful for them, as well as all my past clients, current clients, and those I've yet to meet.

Thank you to my newest family, Ripples Media. Andrew Vogel, Nicole Wedekind, Dorothy Miller-Farleo, Lyn Asman, and Alexa Cole have all been so impactful on my journey and thank you for helping me learn how to write and guide me through the process of publishing the book. Thank you, Mickey Mellon, for the Ripples connection! There was a time in the writing process where I found myself on Shot 8, K.I.T.A. and I wanted to quit. But I had come so far, and I promised I would see it through. Incredibly, that K.I.T.A. pushed me into a mode of writing to a new level, thanks to Andrew!

Thank you to my family, including Jerry and Pat, my parents. Thank you to my brother, Marc. Thanks to my nephew, Maximus, and my cousins John and Reggie. Thanks to my good friends Megan and Mike Amodio for letting me be an "Uncle" to their children. I am grateful to all of you for your support, guidance, friendship, and enthusiasm for this book!

And of course, thank you Bronson. While your ashes float somewhere off a beach near Destin, Florida, your favorite frisbee hangs in a place where it, and you, will never be forgotten.

ABOUT THE AUTHOR

Brent Rittersdorf is a keynote speaker, real estate broker, and Purpose-driven entrepreneur. Originally from Rockland, Maine, and now living in Kennesaw, Georgia, Brent's journey from small-town basketball player to corporate executive to successful entrepreneur embodies the transformative power of understanding your Purpose.

After a distinguished career in the hospitality industry, where he opened over 50 restaurants and managed annual sales exceeding $30 million, Brent transitioned to real estate, becoming a licensed broker in Georgia and Florida. As Managing Broker of High Caliber Realty since 2015, he has built his practice around his core mission: helping clients and their friends make wise decisions in real estate that produce favorable results.

Brent's passion for speaking and teaching grew from his natural preference for being "the guy who pours you the beverage rather than the one ordering it." He has delivered presentations to diverse audiences including restaurant operators, franchisees, entrepreneurs, business associations, and even Officer Candidate School. His signature keynote, "10 for 10," draws from a pivotal high school basketball game where he made all ten free throws in a state semifinal–a moment that would later become the foundation for his life philosophy.

An active community leader, Brent has served as President of the Marietta Business Association and hosts popular networking events that have welcomed over 20,000 attendees. He is also a member of the Kennesaw Business Association and has held leadership roles in Toastmasters International.

This book represents the culmination of Brent's lifelong exploration of what it means to live with Purpose. Through personal stories ranging from corporate boardrooms to real estate closings, from a beloved dog named Bronson to life-changing encounters with clients, Brent provides readers with a practical framework for defining, identifying, and achieving their greater Purpose.

When he's not helping clients navigate real estate transactions or speaking to audiences about Purpose, Brent enjoys mountain biking on Georgia trails and spending time with family in Phoenix and Boston. He continues to believe that everyone deserves to know their Purpose–and that going 10 for 10 is how you achieve it.

www.ingramcontent.com/pod-product-compliance
Lightning Source LLC
Chambersburg PA
CBHW031515120626
46545CB00005B/1887